Praise for

RAISING A KID
WITH SPECIAL
NEEDS

"Being informed is the greatest power someone who is a parent, loved one, or caregiver of an individual living with a disability can possess. Lisa Bendall's *Raising a Kid with Special Needs* is an incredibly comprehensive guide to the information so necessary for families who want to provide their child with the best support and services available to them. It makes me realize how far things have come since my beautiful sister Shanti was little. Bravo!"
GABRIELLE MILLER, STAR OF *CORNER GAS*

"As a leading provider of services for children with disabilities, we welcome this book as an important new resource for Canadians, *Raising a Kid with Special Needs* is sure to become a well-thumbed treasure for many families."
MAX BECK, CEO OF EASTER SEALS CANADA

"I have read your book, and have to tell you how highly readable and family friendly it is. It takes a very large and difficult-to-navigate maze of supports and philosophy related to raising a child with developmental disabilities in Canada and breaks it down into the most profound and impactful pieces for families. Thank you for writing such an important book, which will be welcomed by parents and professionals alike. This will be one book which CDSS will keep in our libraries for a long time."
KRISTA J. FLINT, EXECUTIVE DIRECTOR, CANADIAN DOWN SYNDROME SOCIETY

RAISING A KID
WITH SPECIAL NEEDS

The Complete Canadian Guide

LISA BENDALL

KEY PORTER BOOKS

Library and Archives Canada Cataloguing in Publication

Bendall, Lisa, 1969-
   Raising a kid with special needs : the complete Canadian guide / Lisa Bendall.

Includes index.
ISBN 978-1-55470-018-9

   1. Children with disabilities—Canada. 2. Children with disabilities—Development. 3. Parents of children with disabilities—Canada. I. Title.

HQ773.6.B45 2008   649'.151   C2007-905653-9

ONTARIO ARTS COUNCIL
CONSEIL DES ARTS DE L'ONTARIO

The publisher gratefully acknowledges the support of the Canada Council for the Arts and the Ontario Arts Council for its publishing program. We acknowledge the support of the Government of Ontario through the Ontario Media Development Corporation's Ontario Book Initiative.

We acknowledge the financial support of the Government of Canada through the Book Publishing Industry Development Program (BPIDP) for our publishing activities.

Key Porter Books Limited
Six Adelaide Street East, Tenth Floor
Toronto, Ontario
Canada M5C 1H6

www.keyporter.com

Text design: Marijke Friesen
Electronic formatting: Alison Carr

Printed and bound in Canada

08 09 10 11 12 5 4 3 2 1

To Emily, my cherished crash-course instructor in childrearing,
and Ian, my beloved co-parent and co-pilot

Acknowledgements

From the bottom of my heart I thank the following parents, who were a pleasure to get to know, and who have made such a contribution to others by so honestly telling their stories: Erika Bourque, Leisa DeBono, Roberta Derocher, Linda Dickinson, Mia Fairley, Shelly Garner, Cheri Hearty, Jennifer Huisman, Elizabeth Kreiser, Joan Langevin Levack, Melanie Lepage, Karin Melberg Schwier, Monique Millman, Sherri O'Muir, Stacey Purcell, Julie Robinson, Elouise Simms, Monica Sneath, Debbie Wilson, Annette Walker, Belinda Wright and Sarah Yates-Howorth.

I also wish to express gratitude for the insights and expertise freely shared with me by these professionals: Gary Direnfeld of Interaction Consultants, Dundas, Ontario (www.yoursocialworker.com); Dr. Paulene Kamps of KAMPS: Kinesiology and Meta-Cognitive Psychological Services, Calgary, Alberta (www.drkamps.ca); Jennifer Pym-Murphy of Kawartha Pine Ridge District School Board, Ontario; Dr. Mary Thain of Five Counties Children's Centre, Peterborough, Ontario; and Doreen Wingrove-Burke of Royal University Hospital (NICU), Saskatoon, Saskatchewan.

Last but most definitely not least, I would like to acknowledge the efforts and commitment of Carol Harrison, Linda Pruessen, and the rest of the Key Porter team, who continue to be magnificent to work with, and who in multiple ways have shown their dedication to a full and quality life for all people with disabilities.

Contents

Foreword

BY IAN BROWN

Here is the hard part about reading a book like Lisa Bendall's: She has thought of everything, and you, the parent or sibling or spouse of a disabled person, have not. But here is the good part about a book like this: She really *has* thought of everything.

Someone who thinks of everything is what everyone who takes care of a disabled person wants. The experience of being intimately involved in the life of a disabled child is always an exercise in catching up, a process of reacting. However routine you make it, however organized you are, it's never routine and never organized enough. The simplest tasks are fraught with unpredictable frustrations. And underneath your lurching progress run ever-lurching emotions, too—the steady guilt that afflicts parents of disabled children especially, the spikes of fear that they will be in pain, and of course the steadier drone, the one that never goes away—that you are not doing enough, that there is some relief you have neither sought nor found, that there is (always, always, always) something more you can do.

Raising a Kid with Special Needs is the antidote to those persistent agonies. Lisa has thought about every moment of the experience of raising a handicapped child. She has studied it, she has lived it. Now she has written it down.

All the challenges—from the grandest potential tragedies to the smallest but most meaningful triumphs—are covered in this slim, utterly useful, deceptively important book. Read it. Your life as a caregiver will be a thousand times easier, and richer.

My only regret is that it didn't exist eleven years ago, when my own son was born with a rare disability. Every chapter would have come in handy more or less in the order they appear. The rushing ups and crushing downs of the bewildering process of finding a diagnosis for what my boy had or did not have—and we covered both—would have been laid out ahead of time. The heart-splitting steps of coming to terms with that diagnosis would have been clearly mapped, instead of felt out in a black sadness. Finding a doctor, and then a team or doctors, and navigating a health care system that is cued to crisis, not the chronic? Done. The maddening, stop-and-go process of advocating for your child, and extracting what you need from the system—even items you never imagined you'd need to own, like an IV drip tower? Explained and clarified. The equally demanding search for a school and then the right school and then a better school? Also here, step by step. Taking care of a disabled child is trouble enough. This book takes the guess work out of how.

Then there are all the other parts of your life that need re-organizing because you have been so distracted by your kid's disability. The siblings of a disabled child require a special watchfulness and consideration. So do his or her grandparents, who, as Lisa points out, are probably even more petrified than you are, which is why they never ask if they can help. Ditto your spouse.

And what about your own life, the life of the caregiver? Will it ever again resemble a "normal" life? How much sacrifice is too much? Will you ever again have a moment for a private thought?

The answer is yes. In *Raising a Kid with Special Needs,* Lisa shows you how to find it, seize it, use it.

She also shows you how not to apologise for wanting such a thing. North American society has made immense progress in the way it deals with the disabled—who make up as much as 20 per cent of the population, by one estimate—but the impulse to push them out of sight, to salve our collective conscience by not looking, always lurks close by. Standing up to that willingness to forget, fighting for the rights of your child, requires courage. The clarity of this book, alone, is a form of courage you can ingest like a vitamin.

Even better, Lisa has written something very rare in the vast library of disability writing: a readable and even entertaining book. Who knew it could be done? From the anecdotal and inspiring stories of real lives and real disabilities that launch every chapter—and every reader will find something that speaks to his or her situation, however rare—to her crisp and efficient lists of websites and books that deal with specific problems (it took me four years to find a group that addressed my son's disability), the book is a pleasure to use.

Pay special attention to the lists of suggestions—they're full of gems. Have you ever attended a disability-themed trade show? Thanks to Lisa, I now have—and believe me, they're as entertaining as they are informative. Does the thought of travelling overseas with your handicapped child—and the ton of gear you need to make it even to the corner—fill you with despair? Take heart in the chapter on how to travel.

Do you spend hours wondering if your kid will ever marry? Lisa explains how to increase those odds by developing your child's social skills, as easily as—one of my favorite suggestions—watching people in a mall. Puberty (yikes!) and (eek!) trust funds? The scary future? It's all here. The woman, I tell you, has thought of everything.

Lisa never states them so baldly, but behind every one of her practical suggestions and check lists and resource guides lie profound, vast questions. What is the cost and value of caring for a disabled person? What is just and fair and humane and decent for all concerned? How can we make this deeply satisfying, humanizing and yet harrowing act—looking after a disabled kid—more just and more humane and more decent, for *all* concerned?

It's almost too much to think about. Thank goodness, then, for Lisa Bendel and this book.

—Ian Brown,
Globe and Mail columnist,
January 2008

Introduction

It's estimated that somewhere between 5 and 20 per cent of Canadian families are raising kids with special needs. That means up to one in five families have an inkling of what this is all about.

"Special needs" is a rather woolly expression—after all, *every* kid is special, no?—and later on you'll read about why it might be a better idea to use more definitive terms. But for the purposes of this book, we're talking about those kids who have a disability or disorder that's impressive enough to interfere with basic daily activities like talking, learning, moving about, or fully participating. They may have autism or Asperger syndrome, cerebral palsy or spina bifida, Down syndrome or deafness. Have you ever considered that a child with ADD, severe allergies, or even environmental sensitivities has special needs? If it means your child needs a helping hand with tasks other kids do independently, or if she requires special considerations at school or in the community, then this book is for your family, too.

Whatever your child's disability, it's a good bet your little sugar plum is the utter centre of your universe. And like all parents, you want to do the best by her.

But let's face it, sometimes it's tough to find the information and support you need when your son or daughter happens to have special needs. Sometimes you feel isolated from other parents. Sometimes you feel excluded.

And sometimes you probably wonder if you're even on the right planet.

There's a fabulous fable that's been making the rounds among families raising kids with special needs. It was composed over twenty years ago by Emily Perl Kingsley, an American writer and mom who was raising a boy with Down syndrome.

Kingsley wrote that having a child with a disability is a lot like planning an exciting trip to Italy—complete with guidebooks and language lessons—only to suddenly find out you've landed instead in Holland.

Sure, you're surprised. Definitely disappointed. Maybe a tiny bit terrified out of your wits. You don't know anything about Holland, and you've been dreaming about Italy all your life. Now you have to make new arrangements, learn a new language, hunt down some new guidebooks. It's not at all what you had planned.

But, Kingsley said, after a while you settle in and start to notice what's around you. And guess what? Holland isn't so bad. It's just different. It's even sort of beautiful, and special.

She called her tale "Welcome to Holland."

This story is popular among parents of kids with disabilities because they can relate. Boy, can they: Their trash cans were long ago crammed with so many discarded Italian guidebooks.

But now, take a look at their family albums. The fat pages are filled with stunning, joyful pictures of Holland. Ask them what they think of this foreign country now. They'll say they couldn't imagine being anywhere else.

I was privileged in the writing of this book to connect with parents all across Canada who are raising boys and girls with disabilities. Throughout this book you'll read their stories and hear their insights, born from years of hands-on caring for their kids. They know all about the angst. They'll tell you all about the rapture. In this book you'll also read innumerable tips and useful, practical strategies. And get out your pen—herein are handy lists of all those hard-to-find websites, books, and resources that will help you on your journey. From health care to schooling, from advocacy to future planning, all ages and stages are covered in these pages.

I guess you can consider this your guidebook to Holland.

As you shape the best life you can for your kid, take heart in the knowledge that the future holds all kinds of promise. Today, there are more opportunities than ever before for children and adults with disabilities to become fully participating members of their communities. A 2006 Statistics Canada study shows that 86 per cent of Canadians living with disabilities say they are "pretty happy" or "very happy." In fact, those who have had their disabilities since birth were the happiest of the group. And isn't that all any parent wants for their child?

It's safe to say that your little sweetheart has a bright road ahead. With any luck, this book will provide you with the lowdown you need to make sure she makes the most of her potential—and that the road ahead has as few potholes as possible.

All the best!

IN THE BEGINNING

Dealing with the Diagnosis

1

Meet Claire Kreiser
Lloydminster, Saskatchewan

For many parents, coming to terms with a child's diagnosis is a long road. But Elizabeth Kreiser is one mom who actually accepted the diagnosis before the doctors did.

Elizabeth suspected something was different about her daughter Claire just days after she was born. Her baby girl wasn't crying, nursing, or sleeping well. But she looked the picture of health, and doctors weren't worried.

Mom couldn't let it go. Claire is the youngest of seven kids—four adopted and three biological—so Elizabeth knows from children. Plus her son Joshua had survived bacterial meningitis as a baby and had been shadowed closely by a medical team for years. Elizabeth had learned what to look for in a normally developing child.

Not that anyone took her concerns seriously. "I was convinced that there was something unusual with my baby daughter," says Elizabeth. "But the pediatrician made me feel like an overly doting parent!"

Elizabeth tried another tack. When it came time for one of Joshua's regular physiotherapy appointments at a children's treatment centre, Mom brought along the baby. "I asked the physiotherapist what she thought of Claire's muscle tone," she says. By this time her daughter was a few months old but still didn't lift her head or roll over. "Claire was engaging with her eyes, but she liked to just lie there and not move."

Thankfully the physio agreed this was fishy. At last, Claire was given a referral for the centre's doctors. It took another six months to be seen. "This has always bothered me," says Elizabeth. "Joshua left the hospital with services trailing him. I couldn't keep up with the appointments." Yet with Claire, it seemed the system was in no rush to assess her.

And the answers were still out of reach. The specialists told Elizabeth her baby was delayed but might catch up. "Everyone spoke in roundabout ways," she remembers. "Most said they didn't know."

By the time Claire was a year and a half and still missing milestones, the testing began. Her hearing checked out fine. She tested negative for several known genetic syndromes. "Each time, I'd go on the Internet and read about the thing the geneticist was testing for and shake my head, because it just didn't read like Claire," says Elizabeth. The doctor even considered that an emotional disorder might be the root cause of Claire's delays.

"'Just see how she develops,' the specialists would say. I was thoroughly frustrated," says Elizabeth. "I wasn't sleeping at night because Claire was not sleeping." She scoured the Web for symptoms that sounded like Claire's.

One day, Elizabeth stumbled on a site about Angelman syndrome. She was captivated as she read about the characteristics of this rare disorder. The behaviours, the physical features, the sleep disturbances… "It was totally Claire," she says. The only glitch: The geneticist didn't agree—and refused to test her.

That didn't matter to this mom. "Once I heard about Angelman syndrome, a certain peace came over me. I knew without a doubt that

Claire had it, whether the geneticist would test for it or not." After urging from Claire's pediatrician, though, the test was eventually done.

It was almost anticlimactic when the call finally came: Claire had Angelman syndrome. But at least now Elizabeth had a name for her daughter's differences. And now she could apply her not-insignificant sleuthing skills to learning more about how the syndrome affects Claire.

Today, Claire is a friendly, active seven-year-old who loves the park, relishes mealtimes, and enjoys being invited to her friends' birthday parties. Angelman syndrome is just another side of her.

"We took Claire's diagnosis completely in stride," says Elizabeth now. "We were ready and waiting for it."

"Your child has..."

"Your child is..."

"Your child will always..."

"Your child will never…"

Many parents hold a vivid memory of the day they heard these astonishing words from the lips of some specialist or therapist. At that time, as far as you were concerned, terms like "trisomy 21" or "microencephaly" or "spastic hemiplegia" might as well have been in a foreign language. But today, some of these phrases may have become household words—in your household, anyway.

The group of words that sums up your child's diagnosis are sometimes an important ally, while at other times they feel like a harsh enemy.

Many different types of disabilities and disorders can affect a child's development. Some are congenital (present at birth), like spina bifida or Down syndrome. Some are the result of a premature birth. Others—like cerebral palsy—can be the result of an injury, accident, or illness during labour and delivery, or at some other point during childhood. Still others announce themselves unexpectedly and progressively as a child begins to miss milestones or show symptoms. Autism and learning disabilities are examples of disabilities that often aren't spotted until a child is several months or years old.

Going through the Emotions

Whether you were stunned by an unexpected pronouncement from a pediatrician, or you uncovered your child's condition after years of tests, hearing the actual diagnosis can provoke a range of emotions in a parent:

- **Shock.** You didn't expect it, and it hit you like a tonne of bricks.
- **Vindication.** You've been saying for years there's something different about your kid. You're not crazy after all.
- **Relief.** Now you have a name for it.
- **Anger.** It isn't fair. Your family hasn't done anything to deserve this.
- **Resentment.** Why you? Why didn't this happen to someone else?
- **Fear.** Will your child suffer? Will you be able to handle this?
- **Grief.** You've lost the perfect child you were expecting to have.
- **Denial.** Maybe the doctors made a mistake. Or maybe a miracle cure is in the cards.
- **Anxiety.** What kind of future is in store for your family?
- **Isolation.** None of your friends really understand.
- **Helplessness.** You can't fix this or make it go away.

Great Expectations

So you have a diagnosis. What on earth does it mean? And what can you expect for your child?

- **Get your hands on info.** Find out as much as you can about this disability. When a health care professional talks, take notes. Ask questions. And jump at the chance to attend any workshops or speak to experts. Knowledge will empower you and ease your fears. (See Chapter 3 for more on how to go after information and supports.)
- **Get a second opinion if you want.** Or even a third. Experts can be wrong. But if all the doctors predict the same prospects for your child, chances are they're on target.
- **Talk to parents.** Connect with moms and dads of children with the same diagnosis. Sometimes medical professionals can sound bleak about the future. Experienced parents tell it like it is and, more often than not, are inspiring.
- **Be realistic with your expectations.** You'll only set yourself up for crashing disappointment if your hopes are too high. But do give your kid every opportunity to reach her potential.

Dealing with the Diagnosis

- **No matter what your convictions, be flexible.** Look to your child to take the lead. Through his behaviour, he'll show you when he's ready to grow and learn, and when something isn't working.

About Acceptance

It's not unusual for parents to have a great deal of difficulty coming to terms with their child's diagnosis. After all, this wasn't exactly what you expected when you were expecting! It takes time to adjust. But consider this: The first step in speaking up for your child's rights as someone with a disability is to identify her as a member of this minority. Identifying her also paves a direct path to support services. Don't let your child miss out on programs and professionals that can dramatically boost her quality of life simply because you don't want her to be "one of them."

On the other hand, your child will always be more than his diagnosis. He'll be a redhead. He'll be affectionate. He'll be a leftie. He'll be a big-time fan of spaghetti and meatballs. His diagnosis is just one aspect of an overall terrific kid. Don't let your child become a label, which can be limiting.

Acceptance doesn't usually happen in a eureka moment. It's a process that can take months or even years. And some days are definitely better than others. Don't rush yourself. Allow yourself the time you need to come to terms with your child's special needs.

Living without a Diagnosis

There's a special little waiting room in Label Limbo that's reserved for those parents who have no diagnosis for their children. Living without a diagnosis can be challenging at the best of times. At the worst, it can make you crazy. You have about a zillion unanswered questions. You're frustrated. You may feel as though your concerns about your kid aren't taken seriously. On the other hand, you may have had it up to here with the constant medical tests.

You're not alone. Some disabilities are rare, which makes them harder to identify. Some syndromes are so similar to each other that it can be difficult for specialists to differentiate between them. But you still have the same need for support and services as other parents of kids with special needs. And you can still gain strength by connecting with other families.

Get in Touch
"Living without a Diagnosis"
Contact a Family
Read online at www.cafamily.org.uk/undiagno.html

Canadian Association for Rare Disorders
1-877-302-7273
info@raredisorders.ca
www.raredisorders.ca

Syndromes Without A Name (U.S.)
www.undiagnosed-usa.org

The Guilt Trip

Admit it: You've taken this trip far too many times. Aren't you ready for a change of scenery? There are several reasons why moms and dads of kids with special needs might feel guilty:

- The disability may be the result of a lifestyle choice you made, like drinking during pregnancy.
- You took risks during pregnancy, like taking certain medications or not wearing a seatbelt, resulting in injury to the baby.

- You got pregnant when you were older or in an otherwise high-risk group.
- You chose to move forward with the pregnancy despite the odds that a genetic disorder might be passed down.
- You didn't seek sufficient prenatal care.
- You feel responsible for an illness or injury that happened to your child while under your care.
- You feel responsible for an illness or injury that happened to your child while in the care of someone *you* hired.
- You dyed your hair, ate canned tuna, looked directly at the sun…whatever! We parents are pros at doing guilt. Wouldn't you agree?

Get off the Train

First off, remind yourself that you didn't give your poppet a disability on purpose. Learn to let go of the guilt. And since that's never going to happen—you are a parent, after all—at least find ways to manage it. Some thoughts:

- Don't let your guilt push you to pamper or spoil your child. If you deny him nothing, you won't be doing him any favours. He won't learn to take responsibility for himself.
- Try not to be overprotective. Of course, you want your child to be safe from now on. You don't want any more harm to come to her. But she needs to take small risks and make choices as she gets older, or she'll never learn to be independent.
- Don't set unreasonable expectations. Some parents believe they'll feel less guilty if their child somehow overcomes his disability. Pushing your kid to be a high achiever may only push him toward failure. This child will learn not to try again.
- If you simply can't deal with the guilt, seek counselling. It's in the best interests of both you and your child.

Start Spreading the News

When do you tell your child about his diagnosis, if ever? Only you can make this decision. You know your child best. But whether or not you tell, here are some points to consider:

- If your child asks why she's different or slow, that's a sure sign that it's time to come clean. Don't leave it to her imagination.
- If your child doesn't know he has special needs, he may come up with his own reasons why he has difficulty doing something. He may think he's stupid, or bad. Teaching him about his condition and how it works may work wonders for his self-esteem.
- Make sure your child realizes that her special needs aren't contagious. Sometimes kids worry that their disorders will get worse, or that they'll die, even when this isn't so. Give your child reassurance.
- Bring it down to his level. If he's young, he may not need to know the ins and outs of his genetic neuromuscular disorder. Tell him, in a matter-of-fact tone, that his muscles weren't made strong. As he gets older, add more detail.
- Once she begins to understand her disability, she can start learning how to manage it, and become more empowered. She can develop her strengths and form a self-identity.

 Gold Star Idea

Picture books can be helpful when explaining disabilities to small children. Books can show kids that there are other boys and girls like them. They also equip kids with language that they can use to explain the disability to others. Check your local library or bookstore for stories about your own sweetie's particular special needs. (And see Chapter 6 for some title suggestions.)

Celebrating Your Special Child

You certainly never hoped your half-pint would have disabilities. It's something that happened to you without your bidding. And while, in the beginning, it may seem as though you've been sideswiped by a cyclone, it doesn't mean that every moment of your future family life will be a disaster. In fact, many parents of kids with special needs will tell you that their lives have been vastly enriched by said cyclone. These boys and girls with disabilities have taught them valuable lessons, changed their outlook, pulled the family closer together, or brought them joy.

If you don't believe it, just listen to what these old-timers have to say about what their kids have contributed to their life experience:

"I love my son and don't know where I would be without him. He is special and unique, just like every other child in this world. Just by knowing him, it helps you have respect for other people, with or without disabilities. It makes you aware that life is not perfect and you have to accept what you are given and deal with it, not sit in the corner and cry about things that you cannot change. Our son is loving and funny. I love my son unconditionally and would never, even if given the chance, go back and have a 'normal' child. I cannot imagine my life without him the way he is."

"Loving a child who happens to have special needs is the most insightful journey I will ever take. I was living in a bubble. Until our daughter was born, we had never felt the power of community. We had met our neighbours, but we never felt 'cared for' until challenges faced us. We had meals brought to us regularly during our daughter's prolonged hospital stay, we had offers to help with care for our son, and we had many, many well-wishers contacting us. We suddenly did not feel so alone, and felt that a community was supporting us—something couples sometimes never feel in our day of transitory living. I also learned that no matter how many challenges face us, there is always hope. I learned that human beings are extremely resilient. This realization has been a lovely gift."

"My daughter's disability has been a positive in a lot of ways for me and our family. She has such a strong human spirit. She showed me that even though some of us have disabilities, there is always someone who overcomes more than we can imagine, and that gives us strength and inspiration to go on another day. My daughter has shown me that I am a strong, intelligent woman who has it in me to fight. I have the ability to educate and help others, to support families and meet children and see their abilities, something I do not think I could have ever learned to do without her."

"I have absolutely no doubt that I am a much, much better parent than I ever would have been if my son had been a 'normal' kid. I have learned so much about how to deal with people. I have acquired a whole new vocabulary. I have met so many incredible parents who have inspired me. I have read more books than I ever would have imagined, and it has broadened my understanding of other disabilities. And, yes, our son is a cute, loving, wonderful little kid."

"Our daughter's presence has forced us to re-evaluate what is important in life. When our older children put us through real grief, we thought we had learned it. But when our daughter arrived, I realized that she had a lot to teach all of us as a family. We are blessed that she is a happy little girl who is full of life and loves to be around other people. She has helped break down stereotypes in both our family and the neighbourhood. Everyone knows her and comes up and says hi."

"My son's Down syndrome is probably the best thing that could have happened to me. I am a perfectionist, very hard on myself and those closest to me. My son has taught me to slow down, be patient, and accept him for who he is. All of his accomplishments have made me prouder than I could ever imagine. Of course, I think he is the smartest boy in the world."

"My daughter has been a gift I would never give up. I have become a much stronger and more empathetic person since she has come into my life. Since I've had to be her spokesperson, I have developed those skills and become much better at being a public speaker. I have also learned to be more knowledgeable about disabilities in general. I am much more able to see all sides of situations that come about. She is a great kid, very loving and giving, and gives me at least one laugh per day. I am so thankful that she is in my life."

"Our daughter has a way with people—they seem to be drawn to her. She'll say hi to people shopping in the grocery stores, and gives hugs and kisses to family and friends. She's got a great sense of humour! She and her brother get along great. She worships the ground her big brother walks on, and he adores her. I've heard him educating his friends about Down syndrome. I was so proud of him! I've had strangers come up and talk to me when I'm out and about with my daughter—oftentimes, other parents of kids with Down syndrome. It's a great feeling. She's a charmer, and I couldn't imagine life without her!"

"Our son is always challenging us to be more human, I think. That sounds dumb, but he helps keep our priorities focused just by being with us. By just being here, needing what he needs, he helps our family to think more, plan more, be more aware of *family* now and for the future."

> "I cannot tell you how much my daughter has enriched my life. I feel so lucky."

Get in Touch

Peace Begins with Me: An Inspirational Journey to End Suffering and Restore Joy
By Ted Kuntz

You Will Dream New Dreams: Inspiring Personal Stories by Parents of Children with Disabilities
Edited by Stanley Klein and Kim Schive

Chicken Soup for the Soul—Children with Special Needs: Stories of Love and Understanding for Those Who Care for Children with Disabilities
By Jack Canfield, Mark Victor Hansen, Karen Simmons, and Heather McNamara

Lessons from Jacob: A Disabled Son Teaches His Mother about Courage, Hope and the Joy of Living Each Day to the Fullest
By Ellen Schwartz

General Resources for Diagnosis

Web

"Tips for Parenting a Child with Special Needs"
Bloorview Kids Rehab
Read online at www.bloorview.ca/resourcecentre/familyresources/parenting.php

A Parent's Place: Ideas, Information, and Incidentals for Parents of Children with Developmental Disabilities
www.ualberta.ca/~jpdasddc/parents

Video

They Don't Come with Manuals: Parenting Children with Disabilities
Available from Fanlight Productions (U.S.)
617-469-4999
www.fanlight.com/catalog/films/038_tdcwm.php

Books

Yes You Can! A Guide for Parents of Children with Disabilities
By Mark Nagler
Available from the author's website:
www.marknagler.com/books_by_dr__nagler.htm

Building a Joyful Life with Your Child Who Has Special Needs
By Nancy J. Whiteman and Linda Roan-Yager

Changed by a Child: Companion Notes for Parents of a Child with a Disability
By Barbara Gill

Uncommon Fathers: Reflections on Raising a Child with a Disability
Edited by Donald J. Meyer
Available from Parent Books
1-800-209-9182
www.parentbooks.ca

A Different Kind of Perfect: Writings by Parents on Raising a Child with Special Needs
Edited by Cindy Dowling, Neil Nicoll, and Bernadette Thomas

Breakthrough Parenting for Children with Special Needs: Raising the Bar of Expectations
By Judy Winter

Advocating for Your Child

2

Meet Akasha Cadieux
Ottawa, Ontario

If you look closely at Annette Walker's birth certificate, you just might find out her middle name is "Advocate." This Ottawa mom has been battling on behalf of her child for years.

So which of Annette's five daughters brings out the mother bear in her? That would be eighteen-year-old Akasha, a curly-headed, bright-eyed girl who adores looking at babies (not to mention cute boys). Akasha, also known as Kai (pronounced "Kay"), has a rare global developmental disability. Her exact diagnosis has shifted several times; most recently she is thought to have cerebral folate deficiency syndrome. She's endured tests and treatments, met scores of specialists and social workers. Through it all, Annette has been by her daughter's side, learning as much as she can about Kai's needs and wishes and honing her own advocacy skills.

"I would kill for any of my girls," says Annette. "But with Kai, I would move hell or high water to get what she needs. If I think someone is doing a disservice to her—well, let's just say I'm not a nice person. You don't want to be on the receiving end!"

Back when Kai was born, Annette was a twenty-year-old single mom who, coincidentally, worked with adults with disabilities. These men and women had grown up in institutions and were now adjusting to life in a community they had never known.

"I think this gave me a better insight into what I want for my daughter, compared to what those adults had," Annette says. "I want my daughter to be part of society, to be seen as a human being first."

No one could accuse this mom of having lofty ideals; nevertheless Annette has often faced an uphill struggle. She pushed back against school pressure to place Kai in a special ed class: "I've always been a strong advocate for inclusion. I want her in a regular class doing regular things with regular kids." She doesn't expect her daughter to excel at academics, she says, but she firmly believes the best place for Kai is among her peers. "We call her a lady of leisure— she takes all the easy classes. She loves music. She does art."

Annette often finds herself standing up for Kai when dealing with professionals, too—because she knows Kai's needs better than anyone. "A lot of times I've got so many people involved with her care, and it's overwhelming. But they're coming at it from the perspective of having read it in a book. They've not experienced having a child with a disability."

She's the first to admit that she isn't always as, well, diplomatic as she could be. "I've heard plenty of really ridiculous comments over the years. Sometimes you're just not in the mood to have to explain things to people." But these days, when Annette is ready to let fly with a less-than-civil retort, husband William is often there to help her chill. "He tries to give me the other people's perspectives. Which is good!"

Annette does get weary after years of fighting. "A lot of times, you just want to take her home and hide her away from the world. You just think nobody's ever going to understand." But thanks to her continued efforts, Kai is a happy teenager who enjoys going to high school with her friends, and comes home to a loving family.

"I try to teach people that Kai is a child first and disabled second," says Annette. "If one of her classmates goes on to have a child with a disability, I would like them to look back at Akasha and say, hey, I had a disabled kid in my class and it wasn't that bad.

"Exposure to people like Akasha is what the world needs."

As parents we're often called on to advocate for our kids, whether or not they have special needs. After all, these little tykes are barely half the size of the powerful adults who serve, treat and teach them. And whether folks treat our kids shabbily or whether they shine, they sometimes make decisions that can have a lasting impact on our children's lives. It usually falls to us, the moms and the dads, to make sure the impact is as positive as possible.

When it comes to parenting a child with special needs, you may often find yourself stickhandling the situation when your son or daughter isn't treated equally. Maybe she isn't being extended the same rights or services as other children. Maybe someone speaks to her inappropriately. Maybe the care she's getting just isn't up to snuff. The perpetrators can be total strangers, or they can be teachers, store owners, service providers, relatives, even doctors and specialists.

It can sometimes be exhausting to manage a steady onslaught of slights. But as you regularly go to bat for your bambino, you're doing more than securing his rightful place in society. You're also demonstrating to *him* that he deserves fair treatment. And hopefully, as he grows up, he will feel fully justified in advocating for himself—whether or not you're by his side.

The Many Faces of Advocacy

There's a slew of ways you can stand up for your son or daughter. Sometimes it's subtle, and other times it's about as understated as a stampede across Parliament Hill. The advocacy channels you choose will depend on the situation as well as your child's age and abilities.

- **Make introductions.** Putting a name to your child will help others see your child as an individual and not a disability.
- **Make gentle corrections.** If an usher asks, "Can he see the stage?" invite him to ask your child himself. If a driver says, "Is he confined to a wheelchair?" respond with: "Yes, he *uses* a wheelchair."
- **Share information.** If you want your son's swimming instructor to know more about autism, print out a few pointers. If you'd like the camp leader to learn about seizures, order her a brochure from Epilepsy Canada.
- **Set strangers straight.** You may often find yourself fielding uninvited comments about your kid. You'll need to speak up when someone blurts out, "That poor kid," or "What's wrong with him?" Whether you simply say "He's beautiful the way he is" or "He has a rare disease known as Leber hereditary optic neuropathy. Let me explain how it works"—or something in between—depends on your own comfort level.
- **Just say no.** If you don't think the solution or service being offered is fair to your child, turn it down.
- **Shop around.** Don't stop until you're satisfied your child is being well served, whether it means switching schools or seeking a second opinion from a specialist.
- **Speak with a higher power.** A business owner or manager has more sway than her employees, and is in a better position to make decisions that don't discriminate.
- **Write a letter.** Use the power of the pen to tell a service or business what it's doing wrong, and how you'd like it to improve. Letters are often taken more seriously than verbal complaints.

- **Write articles.** If you've got a propensity for putting things in writing, submit a short item for publication in your local newspaper, school newsletter, or club memo.
- **Learn how to lobby.** Join a group that generates awareness or advocates for positive changes in policy. Stage a protest. Bring local media on side.
- **Make connections.** You'll feel more supported and savvy once you've bonded with other parents in similar situations. It will also help your child to connect to other kids with special needs.
- **Be generous with praise.** When something is done well, say so. Write a letter to pay tribute to the grade two teacher. Tell a storekeeper you appreciate his new automatic door opener.

> **Pearl from a Parent**
> "My belief is that by taking my daughter out in public, everywhere that I go, I am advocating for her. I have never asked if she can be included in anything. I just sign her up and we show up. Believe it or not, I have never had anyone say anything when we show. They just cope with anything that might come up."

The Eight Don'ts of Advocating

1. **Don't come out swinging.** If you adopt an adversarial stance, people will be less likely to want to help you and your child. They may resent your child's needs and even form a negative opinion of them.
2. **Don't let yourself be uninformed—or misinformed.** If you're missing the facts, it's hard to argue your case convincingly. But if you're familiar with the laws, you know your child's rights and you know how the systems work, then you are a potent parent advocate.

3. **Don't assume the rank and file are rude on purpose.** Remember, others may not be as enlightened about certain issues as you are. Perhaps you would have committed the same transgressions in another life.

4. **Don't expect the worst.** If you expect a positive result, your attitude can make a difference in the outcome.

5. **Don't wait for someone else to think of a solution.** Sometimes people are willing to help but don't know how. Since you're the expert on your own child, freely offer suggestions on how she can be accommodated.

6. **Don't disrespect your child.** Avoid saying things like, "My son feels like an idiot in math class because he isn't receiving extra help," or "How do you expect him to find his own way to the bathroom?" You may make your point, but at a cost to your kid's self-esteem.

7. **Don't lose your cool.** If you find you're working your way into a frenzy, walk away. You can always address the issue again later.

8. **Don't pretend to have all the answers.** If you don't have a solution to the problem, feel free to say so. Sometimes others will have creative suggestions.

Get in Touch
"How to Complain Effectively"
Bloorview Kids Rehab
Read online at www.bloorview.ca/resourcecentre/
familyresources/complaining.php

Coaching Kids

It's not just adults who may need to be enlightened when it comes to special needs. Children also may need a little guidance. But thankfully, because they're still forming ideas about the world around them, they're also marvelously open-minded. Here are a few pointers for dealing with a pint-sized inquisition:

- **Don't shush them.** Kids will always have questions, whether it's why your little girl talks funny or why a snow cone melts in the sun. If you hush them up, it will only increase their discomfort around people with disabilities.
- **When explaining special needs, keep it simple and age-appropriate.** Instead of telling a small child all about developmental apraxia, just say, "The muscles in her mouth don't work very well. But she can still understand when you talk to her."
- **Stick to a matter-of-fact tone.** Discuss the disability as if it's no big deal, and the child will learn to see it that way, too.
- **Stress the similarities.** Point out that your son likes to draw too, or that he wants to play soccer this summer.
- **Push the positives.** Let other kids know what your daughter does well. If she's a talented singer, tell them all about it. If she makes her friends feel good with her sunny smile, share this fact.
- **Pick up on opportunities**. If a child is staring, or wanders over with wonder in his eyes, tell him: "This is Sophia. Would you like to say hi to her?"
- **Never force the issue.** If another child is shy about approaching your kid, don't pressure her. You don't want to turn it into a negative experience for her.
- **Teach your child to respond.** Instruct your child to meet an inquisitive stare with a friendly smile, a little wave, or a "Hi." Being goggled at isn't always comfortable, and it will give your kid some control over the situation.

 ## Gold Star Idea

Consider making a storybook to help adults and other kids learn about your child's special needs. Fill the pages with photos of your child playing with the family pet, swimming, or munching birthday cake—the things all kids love to do. Write down normalizing details about your child's life: Is he the only boy in a houseful of sisters? Is lasagna his hands-down favourite meal? Include helpful hints like, "I sometimes yell when I get excited, so please be patient with me," or "I will smile if you sing to me." If your child will be starting day camp or school, this book can be an icebreaker. It can be read aloud in the classroom, and even sent home for other families to borrow.

Know Your Rights

We have several laws in Canada that were written to protect people with disabilities from discrimination. If you get to know them, you'll be armed and ready to defend your child.

- Section 15 of the **Canadian Charter of Rights and Freedoms** guarantees equality to people with disabilities with this wording: "Every individual is equal before and under the law and has the right to the equal protection and equal benefit of the law without discrimination and, in particular, without discrimination based on race, national or ethnic origin, colour, religion, sex, age or mental or physical disability."

- The **Canadian Human Rights Act** outlaws discrimination against people with disabilities by any service provider or employer under its jurisdiction, such as federal government departments, Crown corporations, chartered banks, and national airlines. The Act states: "It is a discriminatory practice in the provision of goods, services, facilities or accommodation customarily available to the general public (a) to deny, or to deny access to, any such good, service, facility or accommodation to any individual, or (b) to differentiate adversely in relation to any individual, on a prohibited ground of discrimination." Every

Canadian province and territory has a similar human rights code prohibiting discrimination in its area of jurisdiction.

- Ontario has a law, the **Accessibility for Ontarians with Disabilities Act**, that covers more ground than any human rights act. Accessibility standards that are developed under this act must be followed by every individual and organization in the public and private sector in the province, although they won't be fully implemented until 2025. Ontario is the first Canadian province to pass this type of legislation.

Get in Touch

Canadian Charter of Rights and Freedoms
Request a print copy by calling 819-956-4802
Or read online at
http://laws.justice.gc.ca/en/const/annex_e.html#I

Canadian Human Rights Act
Request a print copy by calling 819-956-4802
Or read online at http://laws.justice.gc.ca/en/H-6/index.html

Accessibility for Ontarians with Disabilities Act
Request a print copy by calling 1-800-668-9938
Or read online at
www.e-laws.gov.on.ca

Watch Your Language!

When you're talking about your kid's needs, carefully consider the words you use. Saying that your child "suffers" from epilepsy or is a cerebral palsy "victim" makes it sound like her life, well, pretty much sucks. Is that really the impression you want to impart to others? And is it want you want your wee one to hear?

Try to ditch the negative wording by simply saying that your child *has* epilepsy or cerebral palsy. Plus, always make it clear that she's a kid first, and that her diagnosis is secondary. Make a point of saying "my daughter has Down syndrome" instead of "she's a Down's."

Although the expression "special needs" is popular in parenting and schooling circles, and is used throughout this book, it's a euphemism that you may want to reconsider, especially as your child gets older. "Special needs" is a nebulous expression that can have many meanings, while the word "disability" tells it like it is. Plus, the laws that protect your child's rights, the services that support him, and the benefits that he's entitled to when he's an adult are all geared to citizens with "disabilities," not "special needs."

Get in Touch

A Way with Words and Images
Guidelines for the portrayal of persons with disabilities.
Social Development Canada
Request a print copy by calling 1-800-O-CANADA
Read online at
www.hrsdc.gc.ca/en/disability_issues/reports/way_with_words/
page01.shtml

"Disabilities and the Right Words"
B.C. Rehab Foundation
Download free of charge at
www.bcrehab.com/therightwords.html

Teach Your Angel to Advocate

You won't always be there beside your little dumpling to put up your dukes. You can help her learn to stand up for herself by teaching her self-advocacy skills. Here are some tips:

- **She should speak up.** Is she hungry? Does she want her coat off? While she's young, encourage her to get her needs met by asking. This will sow the seeds of self-advocacy later.
- **Be a role model.** Little pitchers have big ears, so set a good example when you advocate. Remember "The Eight Don'ts of Advocating" on page 39.
- **Work on self-esteem.** If he's confident, he'll be comfortable advocating for himself. See Chapter 6 for suggestions to build self-esteem.
- **Give her a show of support.** Talk to her about who the supportive adults in her life are, so she knows who to turn to for help.
- **Pass on the wisdom.** Now that you've become familiar with the rights of people with disabilities, teach your tot.
- **Fools rush in.** Don't be so quick to take over if she's doing okay on her own. She may talk slowly or quietly, but if the other person is still listening, let her go for it.
- **Give him a thumbs-up.** Be sure to praise your little prince when he asserts himself.

Protect Your Child from Abuse

A big part of your job as your child's advocate is to make sure no harm comes to her. Simply by virtue of having a disability, she faces a higher risk than other kids of being abused, whether by a caregiver or by someone else she knows. Your child may be more vulnerable because she has difficulty communicating, or because she needs help to get dressed or go to the toilet, or because she is used to being compliant with health care providers. Abuse can be physical, emotional, or sexual. It can also take the form of neglect.

Below are some strategies for keeping your sweetheart safe. (See also Chapter 8 for help if you feel at risk of abusing your child. See Chapter 10 for more tips on prevention of sexual abuse.)

- Teach your child that he deserves to be treated with respect by every adult he comes into contact with. Tell him he should always talk to you if he isn't treated well.
- During medical appointments and procedures, make sure your child understands what is happening and, as much as possible, co-operates willingly.
- When hiring caregivers, always get several references. Consider doing a police check.
- Pay attention to the way your kid responds to caregivers or other adults in her life. Don't dismiss her reaction—you don't want her to learn to ignore her own instincts.
- Learn the signs of abuse, like extreme behaviour changes, anxiety, regression, or suspicious marks and bruises.
- Always listen to your little one. Let her know she can talk to you and that you won't get mad. (And keep your promise!)

Get in Touch

National Clearinghouse on Family Violence
1-800-267-1291
ncfv-cnivf@phac-aspc.gc.ca
www.phac-aspc.gc.ca/ncfv-cnivf/familyviolence

BOOST: Child Abuse Prevention & Intervention
416-515-1100
info@boostforkids.org
www.boostforkids.org

General Resources for Advocating for Your Child

Organizations

Voices for Children
416-489-5485
cathy@voicesforchildren.ca
www.voicesforchildren.ca

Family Alliance Ontario
905-526-7190
alliance@family-alliance.com
www.family-alliance.com

Web

New Brunswick Association for Community Living
Free online training module: "Advocacy Skills for Families"
www.cnbb.org/nbacl-anbic/index_e.html

Child Parent Disability NetWorks of Manitoba (CPDN)
disability.cimnet.ca/cim/65C100_338T17166.dhtm

Ontario Association of Children's Rehabilitation Services
"Thinking about Advocacy"
www.oacrs.com/resource-familynet-advocacy.php

Books

Reflections from a Different Journey: What Adults with Disabilities Wish All Parents Knew
Edited by Stanley D. Klein and John D. Kemp
Battle Cries: Justice for Kids with Special Needs
By Miriam Edelson

Unfolding the Tent: Advocating for Your One-of-a-Kind Child
By Anne Addison

Advocating for Your Child with Learning Disabilities
Available from the Learning Disabilities Association of Canada
613-238-5721
www.ldac-taac.ca/InDepth/advocacy_toc-e.asp

Parenting Your Complex Child: Become a Powerful Advocate for the Autistic, Down Syndrome, PDD, Bipolar, or Other Special-Needs Child
By Peggy Lou Morgan

Sharing Information about Your Child with Autism Spectrum Disorder: What Do Respite or Alternative Caregivers Need to Know?
By Beverly Vicker

KNOW THE SCORE

Supports, Services, and Information $\quad$ 3

Meet Rebecca Huisman
Calgary, Alberta

Rebecca Huisman may only be three years old, but she knows what she wants. In a nutshell: She wants to do what everyone else is doing. She wants to put on her own socks (and likes helping big brother Owen with his socks, too). She wants to turn the pages of books herself, brusquely shoving aside any helping hands. Even back when she was tube-fed, she'd want to sit at the family dinner table with a dish and a spoon.

"Rebecca is really determined," says her mom, Jennifer. "I think these are traits that are going to take her a long way."

The winsome little girl comes by it honestly. Jennifer and husband Dale have been equally dogged in their pursuit of information and supports, ever since the day their daughter was born with Down syndrome.

Jennifer admits that the early weeks were a blur of medical concerns and prognoses. Although the hospital staff were supportive and met with them frequently to offer advice and answer questions, Jennifer and Dale found it confusing to keep straight all the various community agencies, groups, and programs that were being thrust at them.

But in the years since, the family has got in the game. They've deftly managed to access services, track down resources, and align with a parent group. They've also found renewed warmth and support in their community. "Everywhere I go now, I find a friendly face," Jennifer says.

Connecting with other parents of kids with Down syndrome has been a huge help, says Jennifer. Rebecca was two weeks old when Jennifer first heard from another mom who knew exactly what she was going through. "We gabbed on the phone. She told me about her son, who was the love of her life." She adds: "I gained so much from just talking to these parents. You just realized there was a huge community of people out there who were willing to help you out. The more you spoke, the more you found out you were not alone."

The support services offered to her by disability agencies also helped Jennifer feel less isolated. "When you're used to being fairly self-sufficient, you think you can tackle problems all on your own. You think that if you read enough books, and put enough time into it, you'll fix them," she says. "With Rebecca I thought, this is my child. I really shouldn't be feeling overwhelmed." But by letting Jennifer know that she was eligible to receive assistance, these agencies handed her the validation she needed. They effectively enabled her to accept help.

Jennifer relies on the Internet as a useful tool, as well. When doctors told her Rebecca had congenital laryngomalacia (an abnormality of the windpipe), she used a search engine to learn more about it. When Rebecca struggled with constipation because of her low muscle tone and difficulty taking in fluids, her mom went online for ideas. She stresses that she's careful not to believe everything she reads on the Web. "But if I do see consensus online, I use it as a sort of primer before I go in to see the doctor," she says. "Quite often, it's written in layman's terms."

As parents, Jennifer and Dale have become pros at finding the supports they need. But at the end of the day, their focus is on their family. When Rebecca first came home from the hospital at three weeks of age, recalls Jennifer, "We had this weight on our shoulders." Their three-year-old son gave them the lift they needed. "Owen looked over at his baby sister adoringly and said, 'We have the best baby in the whole world.'" True, Owen may not always feel the same way now, especially when his little sister is messing with his toy pirates. But those are words his parents will never forget.

"It was a good starting point for all of us," Jennifer says. And the rest is history.

When you first discovered your son or daughter has a disability, you might have felt very alone. But the truth is, there's a world of resources out there waiting for you. The key is knowing how and where to access them. Many parents describe feeling overwhelmed by the options, with the names of similar-sounding programs and agencies blurring together in their minds. Others talk about how years of their child's life had gone by before they finally stumbled upon an essential support service right in their own community.

Information is power, so the more you can gather, the stronger you will be in your role as a parent to your special child.

Disability Organizations

A variety of different disabilities and disorders can affect kids. They can have an impact on kids' growth and development, their learning abilities, their mobility, speech, hearing, and vision. Fortunately, there are hundreds of non-profit organizations set up across the country with the primary purpose of providing information and support to families.

In your quest to know the score, often a disability-specific organization is your best bet for a first stop. Here you can get answers to your general questions, find out about services and products, hear about upcoming events like workshops or conferences, order brochures, and even swap personal stories and inspiration. Some groups offer more benefits for a modest membership fee. Head for the national headquarters of these organizations, and you'll often find local chapters listed that may offer lectures and services in your own community.

For a list of organizations addressing the most common causes of disability among Canadian kids, see the end of this chapter.

Where Else Can You Get the Scoop?

- **Connect with peer parents.** Swap what you know with other moms and dads who are raising kids with disabilities. If their child is older than yours, chances are they already know how to fast-track those funding applications or plot out those parent-teacher meetings. Consider joining or even starting up a parent support group in your community.
- **Catch up on your reading.** Many organizations for specific disabilities, such as the Learning Disabilities Association of Canada or the Canadian Diabetes Association, publish regular newsletters with updates, tips, and personal stories. Often, back issues are available on organization websites. *Abilities* is a positive cross-disability magazine with a range of articles and resources.
- **Join online forums or listservs.** From the comfort of your computer room at home, read or exchange messages about parenting a child with a disability. Many parenting websites, such as TodaysParent.com, offer active forums dedicated to families with special needs where you can discuss treatments,

ask questions, or lend support. Some organizations, like the Canadian Down Syndrome Society, host parent forums that are more disability-specific.

- **Participate in conferences and seminars.** Many disability organizations offer workshops aimed at parents. Often they're free of charge. Not only can you learn how to help your little one, but you can also take the opportunity to network with other moms and dads.
- **Attend disability-themed trade shows.** Some of the more size-able Canadian cities host annual events where you can peruse new products and equipment or find out about services. The largest is People in Motion in Toronto. Rehab Equipment Expo, in Vancouver, is the biggest in western Canada.
- **Keep in touch with advocacy groups.** Join mailing lists or log on to disability advocacy websites to stay in the loop about changes in legislation or petition signings.

Get in Touch

Differences in Common: Self-Help for Parents of Children with Special Needs
By Janice MacAulay
Read online at www.cfc-efc.ca/docs/cafrp/00001112.htm

Abilities
Published by the Canadian Abilities Foundation
416-923-1885
info@abilities.ca
www.abilities.ca

Exceptional Parent magazine (U.S.)
1-877-372-7368
epar@kable.com
www.eparent.com

NATIONAL

Published by the Learning Disabilities Association of Canada

613-238-5721

information@ldac-taac.ca

www.ldac-taac.ca

UpDate

Published by the Spina Bifida and Hydrocephalus Association of Canada

1-800-565-9488

info@sbhac.ca

www.sbhac.ca

TodaysParent.com

www.todaysparent.com/community/forums/?families_with_special_needs

CanadianParents.com

forum.canadianparents.com/ubbthreads/ubbthreads.php?ubb=postlist&Board=33&page=1

Baby Center

www.babycenter.ca/baby/specialneedsboardcanada

People in Motion

1-877-745-6555

www.people-in-motion.com

Rehab Equipment Expo (REE)

604-737-6410

ian.denison@vch.ca

Council of Canadians with Disabilities
204-947-0303
ccd@ccdonline.ca
www.ccdonline.ca

Notes about the Net

No question, the Internet is an invaluable source of information and support. Where else could you stumble across Braille-shaped blocks for teaching a blind child to read? How else could you befriend a mom in Moscow whose daughter's diagnosis could have been lifted from your own kid's medical file? From products to breakthroughs to pen-pal matches made in heaven, the Internet dishes up a smorgasbord. But before you get too smitten with cyberspace, do remember:

- Don't believe everything you read! Many websites contain information and articles posted by people with no medical or professional training. What they've written may reflect their opinion, but nothing more.
- Get familiar with the "About Us" buttons on the websites you visit. This will tell you who's behind them. If the information comes from a reputable organization, university, hospital, or clinic, chances are it's reasonably reliable.
- Never start your child on treatment or therapies based solely on something you've read online. Always check in with your child's health care provider.
- Even if Internet information is accurate, that doesn't mean it applies to your individual child. Every situation is different.
- Never give out your personal information on the Internet unless you know how it will be used—and protected.

ﾡ hand? Once you start building your network and gathering information, you'll find there's a wide range of resources in your community that can be of help to your family. Many services are government-funded and free. Others are offered by non-profit agencies at little or no cost to you. Some sources of support are privately managed and charge fees accordingly. It's up to you, together with your child's health care provider, to decide what's best for your bambino. The aim of these services is to help your child reach her full potential. Here's a sampling of what's out there:

- **Early intervention or infant development therapy.** These services can enhance your child's development in many areas, including sensory skills, social skills, and cognition.
- **Occupational therapy or physiotherapy.** These therapies promote physical development.
- **Speech therapy.** Speech-language pathologists can help your child improve his pronunciation and use of speech.
- **Respite care.** No question that raising a child with special needs is a 24/7 job. Respite is short-term care that allows Mom or Dad to have a break.
- **Home care or attendant services.** Home care workers can assist your child with tasks like getting bathed and dressed.
- **Music therapy.** Music can help kids develop their communication skills, self-awareness, and self-esteem.
- **Play therapy.** This can help to ease anxiety issues, lessen behaviour problems, or boost social skills. The service can be delivered formally by a professional play therapist, or it can happen more naturally in a structured play-group setting.
- **Tutoring or homework help.** If your child has learning disabilities, specialized tutoring can pick up where the regular classroom leaves off.

- **Support workers.** Your child may require assistance at day camps and recreational programs in order to fully participate.
- **Service dogs.** These first-class critters can guide kids with vision disabilities, protect kids with autism from danger, and even keep kids with epilepsy safe.

> **Pearl from a Parent**
> "Most invaluable to me now is home care, which provides time away for both my daughter and I, and enables us to enjoy our time together, despite the caring responsibilities which continue."

Buyer Beware

- **For government-funded programs,** waiting lists in many parts of the country are long. So don't drag your feet when it comes to putting in the call.
- **Some, but not all, programs are income-based.** That means if your household income is above a certain threshold, you won't be eligible. Or you may pay based on a sliding scale.
- **If you live in a remote community,** you may not have all the services you need close at hand. But some provinces will provide funding to help cover transportation costs.
- **Programs and services can sometimes be tied together.** You can't take one without the other. This can sometimes narrow the options that fit your family.
- **Insurance plans vary widely in terms of what they'll cover.** Be sure to find out more about yours before you shell out for services.
- **Private services can put you out of pocket.** So before you sign up, scope it out!

Supports, Services, and Information

Get in Touch

Children and Youth with Special Needs Branch
B.C. Ministry of Children and Family Development
250-952-6044
mcf.childrenyouthspecialneeds@gov.bc.ca
www.mcf.gov.bc.ca/spec_needs

Community Based Services for Children with Special Needs
New Brunswick Family and Community Services
506-453-2001
www.gnb.ca/0017/Disabilities/index-e.asp

Children's Special Services
Manitoba Family Services and Housing
204-945-1042
www.gov.mb.ca/fs/pwd/css.html

Early Intervention Nova Scotia
902-354-5890
inquiries@earlyintervention.net
www.earlyintervention.net

Canadian Association for Music Therapy
1-800-996-CAMT
camt@musictherapy.ca
www.musictherapy.ca

Canadian Association for Child and Play Therapy
1-800-361-3951
membership@cacpt.com
www.cacpt.com

National Service Dogs
519-623-4188
info@nsd.on.ca
www.nsd.on.ca

Get the Goods

Supports for your kid with special needs don't only come in the form of therapies and assistants. Sometimes it's stuff, not services, that can make daily living a little easier. In fact, more than two-thirds of Canadian school-aged kids with disabilities need some sort of aid or assistive device. But almost half of them don't have every device they need. Maybe that's because it's hard to find, or it costs too much. Maybe the child won't use it often enough to make it seem worthwhile. Don't let any of that stop you! Use your growing information network to get your hands on the gizmos that can make a difference to your kid. Read Chapter 9 for funding ideas. Disability products include:

- **Mobility aids** such as wheelchairs, walkers, crutches, orthopedic shoes, and braces.
- **Assistive devices** such as hearing aids, easy-grip spoons, potty seats with armrests, and wheelchair trays.
- **Computers and technology** such as enlarged keyboards, learning software, talking books, and electronic speaking devices.
- **Home health care supplies** such as catheters, feeding tube supplies, diapers, disposable gloves, and wipes.
- **Home modifications** such as lifts, grab bars, and lever faucets.
- **Vehicle modifications** such as ramps and wheelchair tie-down systems.

Gold Star Idea

Do it yourself! Not every assistive product has a price tag. To help your child learn to recognize the alphabet, make tactile letters by cutting out shapes from coloured paper and gluing on rice or lentils. Adding Velcro to pants, instead of zippers, may spell the difference between whether or not your child can use the bathroom by herself. You can even adapt your own battery-operated toys with accessible on-off switches.

Get in Touch

The Motion Group
Thirty-two affiliated outlets across Canada.
1-888-850-9188
www.themotiongroup.com

Northland Healthcare Products Ltd.
Four store locations in Winnipeg.
204-786-6786
www.nhcp.com

Easter Seals New Brunswick Equipment Recycle Program
506-458-8739
www.easterseals.nb.ca

Computer Resources for People with Disabilities: A Guide to Assistive Technologies, Tools and Resources for People of All Ages
Available from the Alliance for Technology Access (U.S.)
707-778-3011
www.ataccess.org

Hey! Can I Try That? A Student Handbook for Choosing and Using Assistive Technology
By Gary Bowser and Penny Reed
Wisconsin Assistive Technology Initiative
Read online at www.wati.org/products/pdf/heycanitrythat.pdf

Shoppers HomeHealthCare
Over sixty centres across Canada. Find a store near you at:
www.shoppersdrugmart.ca/english/home_health_care
or call 1-800-SHOPPER (1-800-746-7737)

Tetra Society of North America
Matches volunteer engineers and technicians with people with disabilities who are in need of creative assistive devices.
1-877-688-8762
info@tetrasociety.org
www.tetrasociety.org

Workshop Solutions
An online directory of home-built assistive devices.
www.workshopsolutions.com

Adapt My World: Homemade Adaptations for People with Disabilities
By J. Rose Plaxen

Life Support

Some types of assistance you won't find at a store or in a service directory. Don't forget to turn to these sources of support when you need them. Often the other adults in your life want to do something, but are short on ideas. It's up to you to ask for help.

- **Relatives.** Chances are, your in-laws would be delighted to spend an afternoon with your baby while you relax in a long-overdue bubble bath (okay, let's be honest—while you pay those long-overdue bills).
- **Neighbours.** If you haven't gotten to know the folks on your block, now's the time—especially if they have kids, too, and you can swap child care with them.
- **Friends.** You were there for your gal pal when she split up with her soul mate, so call in a favour: Let hers be the shoulder you cry on when you need it. Failing that, let her do your laundry.

Pearl from a Parent

"Accepting help from non-professionals like friends and neighbours has been a great challenge for me. I came to realize that many people feel strongly about the trying situations of others, and reach out by offering to help. Provided they are not taken advantage of, they feel good about doing simple things like dropping off a dinner or providing a playdate for a sibling. I have now learned to accept help and return the favours when I am able—either to the same people or someone new."

Sweet Dreams

In your endeavour to make sure your child's health and developmental needs are met, don't forget to meet her need for fun. Some non-profit organizations are set up to fulfill a child's special dream or wish. The goal is to help these kids forget painful procedures or deal with harsh medical treatments. (Note: For some programs, only children with life-threatening conditions are eligible.) For more on giving your kids a high old time, see Chapter 6 for recreational ideas.

Get in Touch

Sunshine Dreams for Kids
1-800-461-7935
info@sunshine.ca
www.sunshine.ca

A World of Dreams Foundation Canada
1-800-567-7254
info@awdreams.com
www.awdreams.com

Children's Wish Foundation of Canada
1-800-267-9474
linda.marco@childrenswish.ca
www.childrenswish.ca

Make-A-Wish Foundation of Canada
1-888-822-9474
nationaloffice@makeawish.ca
www.makeawish.ca

Glossary of Disabilities

• Asthma and allergies

Asthma causes inflammation in a child's air passages. Symptoms are often triggered by moulds, smoke, even cold air or exercise. Certain allergies can cause anaphylaxis, a severe reaction that requires immediate treatment.

Asthma Society of Canada
1-866-787-4050
info@asthma.ca

www.asthma.ca
For kids and parents: www.asthma-kids.ca

Allergy/Asthma Information Association
1-800-611-7011
national@aaia.ca
www.aaia.ca

• Autism spectrum disorders

Autism is a neurological disorder that can affect a child's development, behaviour, and social and communication skills. Pervasive developmental disorder (PDD) and Asperger syndrome are two other disorders in the autism spectrum.

Autism Society Canada
613-789-8943
info@autismsocietycanada.ca
www.autismsocietycanada.ca

• Cerebral palsy

Cerebral palsy (CP) is caused by damage to the brain immediately before, during, or after birth. This damage interferes with the brain's ability to send and receive messages, so a child with CP may have difficulty controlling parts of her body. The brain injury can also cause cognitive disabilities.

Ontario Federation for Cerebral Palsy
1-877-244-9686
info@ofcp.on.ca
www.ofcp.on.ca

Cerebral Palsy Association in Alberta
1-888-477-8030

info@cpalberta.com
www.cpalberta.com

• Developmental, intellectual, or cognitive disabilities
Many different conditions can affect a child's intellectual func-
tioning, causing him to learn, concentrate, reason, develop, or
participate socially at a below-average level. Sometimes the
cause of an intellectual disability is completely unknown.

Canadian Association for Community Living
416-661-9611
inform@cacl.ca
www.cacl.ca

• Diabetes
Type 1 diabetes is one of the most common chronic diseases in
kids. The bodies of these children don't make enough insulin to
keep their blood glucose levels in check. As they get older, other
secondary disabilities can sometimes develop.

Canadian Diabetes Association
1-800-226-8464
info@diabetes.ca
www.diabetes.ca

• Down syndrome
Down syndrome is a genetic condition, the result of a variation
on the twenty-first chromosome. Kids with Down syndrome have
some degree of cognitive disability, and may have other health or
developmental conditions as well.

Canadian Down Syndrome Society
1-800-883-5608

info@cdss.ca
www.cdss.ca

• Environmental sensitivities

Some children become ill when they're exposed to common substances in their homes, communities, or schools like perfumes, paint, and detergent. The families of these kids often have to take care to avoid places and situations where they might get sick.

Allergy and Environmental Health Association of Canada
613-860-2342
office@aeha.ca
www.aeha.ca

• Epilepsy and seizure disorders

Epilepsy is a neurological condition that can result from brain injury or infection, but often has an unknown cause. About half of all kids with epilepsy will grow out of their seizures.

Epilepsy Canada
1-877-734-0873
epilepsy@epilepsy.ca
www.epilepsy.ca

• Fetal alcohol syndrome/effects

Children with fetal alcohol syndrome may have a range of developmental disabilities resulting from exposure to alcohol before birth.

Fetal Alcohol Spectrum Disorder (FASD) Information Services
Canadian Centre on Substance Abuse
1-800-559-4514
fas@ccsa.ca
www.ccsa.ca/CCSA/EN/Topics/Populations/FASD.htm

• Hearing disabilities

Kids can have mild hearing loss, be profoundly deaf, or be somewhere in between. Hearing aids, sign language, and cochlear implants are some of the approaches that can make a difference.

Canadian Hearing Society
1-877-347-3427
info@chs.ca
www.chs.ca

• Heart disease

It's not just elderly folks who contend with heart conditions. About one in one hundred kids is diagnosed with heart disease each year. Children can be born with heart disease, or they can develop it at a later age.

The Children's Heart Society
1-888-247-9404
childrensheart@shaw.ca
www.childrensheart.org

• Learning disabilities

Learning disabilities affect the way a child takes in, understands, or remembers information. Some examples include attention deficit hyperactivity disorder and dyslexia. A learning disability is not related to intellect.

Learning Disabilities Association of Canada
613-238-5721
information@ldac-taac.ca
www.ldac-taac.ca

• Mental health disabilities

Children can experience mental health–related disabilities like obsessive-compulsive disorder, anxiety, and depression. These disorders can make it difficult to cope with school and activities.

Canadian Mental Health Association
416-484-7750
info@cmha.ca
www.cmha.ca

• Muscular dystrophy

Muscular dystrophy, or neuromuscular disorder, is a disability in which muscle tissue gradually becomes weaker or wastes away. As it progresses, children have more difficulty walking, using their hands, or sometimes even speaking. There are more than a hundred types of neuromuscular disorders.

Muscular Dystrophy Canada
1-866-MUSCLE-8
info@muscle.ca
www.muscle.ca

• Rare disorders

Did you know one in ten Canadians has a rare disorder? Parents of kids with uncommon conditions have unique challenges. Whether your child has Pallister-Hall syndrome or hemimega-lencephaly, you'll have more difficulty finding organizations, parent groups, or books on the topic, let alone national fundraising campaigns and research teams.

Canadian Association for Rare Disorders
1-877-302-7273
info@raredisorders.ca
www.raredisorders.ca

• **Speech and communication disabilities**

This group of disorders includes stuttering, apraxia, selective mutism, and some learning disabilities. Many speech disorders are the result of other disabilities, such as cleft palate or Down syndrome.

Canadian Association for People Who Stutter
1-888-STUTTER
csa@stutter.ca
www.stutter.ca

Ontario Association for Families of Children with Communication Disorders
519-842-9506
www.oafccd.com/main.htm

• **Spina bifida and hydrocephalus**

If a kid has spina bifida, that means her spine has not formed properly. It results in a damaged spinal cord and some degree of paralysis. Children with spina bifida often also have hydrocephalus, which means the fluid in their brains does not drain properly and creates pressure.

Spina Bifida and Hydrocephalus Association of Canada
1-800-565-9488
info@sbhac.ca
www.sbhac.ca

• **Vision disabilities**

Only a small number of Canadian kids have vision disabilities. That means that it can sometimes be difficult to find support and information for them. Whether a child is completely blind or has partial vision, he may need extra support in areas like literacy.

Canadian National Institute for the Blind

1-800-563-2642

info@cnib.ca

www.cnib.ca

General Resources for Supports, Services, and Information

Organizations

Family Network for Deaf Children

604-684-1860

fndc@fndc.ca

www.fndc.ca

Special Needs Adoptive Parents (SNAP)

604-687-3114

info@snap.bc.ca

www.snap.bc.ca

Hotlines

Child Disability Resource Link

Information and referral to a range of Alberta government and community supports and services for children with disabilities.

1-866-346-4661

Web

Persons with Disabilities Online
www.pwd-online.ca

LiNKd.org: Linked Information for Kids with Disabilities in
Manitoba
www.umanitoba.ca/outreach/linkd

Canadian Directory of Genetic Support Groups
www.lhsc.on.ca/programs/medgenet

Internet Resources for Special Children (U.S.)
http://www.irsc.org:8080/irsc/irscmain.nsf

Special Child: For Parents and Caregivers of Children with
Special Needs (U.S.)
www.specialchild.com

Books

*Disabilities, Dragons and Other Magical Discoveries: A Kid's
Guide to Understanding and Living with Disabilities*
By Rick Enright
Available from Thames Valley Children's Centre
519-685-8680
www.tvcc.on.ca

*Disability is Natural: Revolutionary Common Sense for Raising
Successful Children with Disabilities*
By Kathie Snow

Supports, Services, and Information

A Parent's Guide to Developmental Delays: Recognizing and Coping with Missed Milestones in Speech, Movement, Learning, and Other Areas
By Laurie Fivozinsky LeComer

Film

ASD...Heads Up for the Low Down
Current information on autism spectrum disorders.
Available from Program Development Associates (U.S.)
1-800-543-2119

The Health Care System and Healthy Living

4

Meet Madeline Gibbons
Colborne, Ontario

Madeline Gibbons is a busy seven-year-old. She loves chasing her two cats around and wrestling with her brother. She likes looking at books and playing tea party. And let it be known that this girl is a music fan with eclectic tastes—she'll bop to anything from Johnny Cash to Dido to Sharon, Lois and Bram.

These days, Maddy is enjoying good health and takes no medications. But as a baby she was desperately sick. Born with a serious heart defect associated with her Down syndrome, she went into heart failure at two weeks of age. Then she developed an E. coli infection while still in the neonatal intensive care unit. (Not to be outdone, her brother Joshua came down with the chicken pox at home.) "I was at my wit's end," remembers her mom, Monique Millman, who made the three-hour round trip to the hospital every day—while still recovering from a C-section—so she could spend time with both her children.

Although frantically worried, Monique focused all her attention on her new daughter during her hospital visits. "We cuddled, and I changed her diapers," she says. "We bonded nicely." Monique brought in toys, photos, and music to play to Madeline, and she talked to her. And often cried.

"At first it was draining," Monique says of the daily commute. "But I did get used to it after a while. It was almost like going to a job."

Even jobs come with days off, though, and Monique confesses to slacking off occasionally. "I allowed myself a break," she says. "I sent my mom to be with Madeline. I was able to relax a bit and spend some time with my son." She adds that these rare respites helped her spirits tremendously.

In fact, her family proved to be an important source of support. Having one child in hospital usually means scrambling to find care for the other. It helped that Monique's parents live just a couple of doors away in their rural community. Most of her friends came through for her, too, Monique recalls, and she can't say enough about the first-rate sitter who picked up the slack. "We just enlisted the army," she laughs.

Another set of troops could be found at the hospital. Monique drew strength from them as well. "The nurses there were very, very supportive," she says. One particular social worker, whom Monique has dubbed her "saviour," often gave her a shoulder to cry on. "It was such a roller-coaster ride of emotions," Monique adds.

Fortunately, Madeline's heart was successfully repaired when she was fourteen weeks old, and the tiny girl grew stronger. She was tube-fed for almost a year, but now, at age seven, Maddy can down pepperoni pizza with the best of 'em. The frail little newborn who fought for her life is now thriving.

Not that Madeline doesn't keep in touch with an array of health professionals. Monique regularly drives her daughter into town for cardiology, physiotherapy, and speech therapy appointments. Because they live in a rural area, these excursions can be exhausting.

Maddy might face surgery in the future to correct a mitral valve regurgitation in her heart, but in the meantime she's robust and rambunctious. She's spoiled silly by her stepfather, Johnny, says Mom, and she's doted on by classmates. She and her brother play together often and get along like bread and butter.

"I hope that she's not going to have any more heart issues," says her mom. "That's the biggest thing."

When it comes to your child, no commodity is more precious than her health. Some kids with special needs see their doctors so often they ought to be on a frequent-flier program. Many other children with disabilities, however, enjoy sound health and see their practitioners no more frequently than other kids.

Whether your child is medically fragile or hale and hearty, a disability can sometimes complicate a routine check-up or dentist visit. It can even mean that basic health needs like nutrition and fitness become more of a challenge.

Choosing a Health Care Provider

It can be tough to decide on just the right doctor for your child. But consider yourself lucky if you're faced with a choice: In many parts of Canada, where waiting lists are long, you take what you can get. If you do have options, here are a few questions to keep in mind as you make your selection.

- **Does the doctor** have expertise in your child's particular special needs? If not, will he readily make referrals to specialists when you need them?
- **Has she been recommended** by someone you know and trust?

Extra points if the referral comes from another parent of a child with a disability.

- **How does he behave** with your child? Does he treat your daughter as the adorable little girl she is, or as a medical condition first?
- **Does your child seem comfortable** with the doctor? (Keep in mind, though, that some kids just don't warm up to doctors of any type—even Elmo in a lab coat would set them screaming!)
- **Does she take time with you?** Does she learn about your child by listening to you?
- **In general,** how quickly will you be able to get an appointment for your kid when you call?
- **Do the office hours work for you?** What happens when the doctor is on vacation? Is there a back-up available?
- **Is the waiting room comfortable?** Are there toys and books to distract your kid when she's climbing the walls? You might be spending a lot of time here, and the last thing you need is a bored or restless child.
- **If your child uses** a wheelchair or other mobility aid, are the physician's examining rooms accessible? How about the washroom? Is the examining table height-adjustable to help with transfers when your child is bigger? You may be able to scoop up your sweetie now, but in ten years' time the transfers will be trickier.
- **Is the doctor open-minded** about complementary treatments such as chiropractic or dietary supplements, should you choose to explore them?
- **Will the doctor consider** giving advice over the phone? How about prescription refills?

Get in Touch
"Choosing Your Child's Doctor"
By William Feldman, MD
Read online at
www.canadianparents.com/article/choosing-your-childs-doctor

Dealing with Doctors

So you've settled on a health care team for your child? Your diligence shouldn't end here. There are ongoing ways you can ensure that your encounters with the medical system are smooth sailing.

- **Write down** your questions before an appointment.
- **Bring a pen and notepad** so you can jot down new information. Remember, the doc is probably more likely to dish if he sees that you're an active listener. And you'll have total recall when you need it.
- **Try to arrange for the same parent** to be at all appointments— or have both parents attend.
- **Resist ranting about a previous doctor's treatment**. It won't help your current doctor to hear this, and it may make her wary about working with you.
- **Try not to be critical of your current doctor.** Be open-minded and well-mannered so that dealing with your family is a pleasant experience for him. Your little one is liable to benefit from more conscientious care.
- **Ask for solutions.** After all, you have a better handle on your kid's day-to-day state than the doctor does. If you think your child has been in pain or distress, be sure to communicate this to the health care provider.
- **Don't be shy about sharing your expertise.** You know more about your child than anyone. Do injections upset her? Is she better with liquids than pills? A backgrounder can go a long way towards helping the doctor help your kid.
- **Be honest** about what medical advice is being followed at home—and what isn't. Your child's therapist needs to know if the exercises she recommended just aren't fitting in to your family's routine. She may have other suggestions.
- **Ask for extra copies** of all medical reports and records, including specialists' notes that would normally be sent directly to your

child's GP. And make sure you can decipher them! If you're not sure what a particular phrase means—or if you can't read the doctor's chicken scratch—speak up.

- **Be sweet to the secretary.** When it comes to appointments that suit your schedule, reports that need faxing, and tests that need follow-up, she's the gatekeeper. So it's worth your while to enlist her as your ally.
- **Acknowledge your emotional state.** It's natural to be nervous, worried, or frightened before or during your child's medical appointments and procedures. Recognize that this may affect your ability to remember what the doctors tell you, or to rattle off important information about your child's medications. All the more reason to keep careful notes!
- **Get to know your pharmacist**. She's not your doctor, but she does dispense the drugs. If she gets familiar with your child's history and other medications he's taking, she may prove to be another good source of guidance.
- **Trust your instincts.** If you aren't comfortable with your kid's treatment, speak up or seek another opinion. But be honest about what's best for your little one, even if it's outside your comfort zone.

Your Best Friend the Binder

Parents and doctors agree: A grade-A way to stay organized is with a binder that holds the details of your child's entire medical history. Don't rely on your memory, which as any parent knows can fail you at the best of times. Always have the facts at your fingertips. Here's what to include:

- Copies of medical reports and assessments.
- Dates of all appointments and surgeries, along with your notes about the outcomes.

- A list of known drug reactions and food allergies.
- Your child's current height and weight.
- An inventory of all medications your child is taking, including dosage. Don't expect the doctor to know what you mean by "the orange one that comes in a bottle." Include non-prescription medicines, herbal remedies, and vitamin supplements on this list.
- A list of all doctors and specialists you're dealing with. If your child was treated by a resident in a teaching hospital, be sure to write down the name of the supervising doctor on staff, even if you never laid eyes on her.

 ## Gold Star Idea

Kids with disabilities are more likely to have dental problems, for a variety of reasons, from difficulty chewing to having to swallow a lot of sweetened medications. So don't be lax about looking after your child's teeth. If you can, do the dental visits in installments: Schedule shorter, more frequent visits to the dentist's chair instead of long, drawn-out—and potentially agonizing—appointments. (Most insurance plans will put a cap on the amount of dental work you have done, but not on the number of appointments involved.) And this "short and sweet" strategy may help to ease fears and keep your kid engaged.

Coping with a Kid in Hospital

It's tough when your little tyke has to spend time in hospital, whether it's just overnight or for an extended period. Here are some tips for easing the experience:

- **Some hospitals** have pre-admission programs that give kids a chance to take a tour—or a virtual tour from home—and learn what to expect. These children are often less anxious when it comes to surgery day.

- **Special toys, books, and family photos** in your sweetie's suitcase will help her feel more comfortable staying away from home.
- **Don't forget to pack** all of your child's medications.
- **If you have other kids**, make sure you're comfortable with your child-care arrangements. It's difficult to give all your focus to your hospitalized child if you're fretting about the rest of your family.
- **Let the nursing staff know** about your child's particular abilities, likes and dislikes, and needs.
- **Be aware** that because of your child's condition, she may not have typical responses to things like sedation and recovery.
- **Familiar routines** like playtime and lullabies will help your child adjust to the hospital stay.
- **Consider staying overnight,** if the hospital will accommodate you. Your very presence will go a long way to ensuring your kid gets good care. It will also be reassuring for your child to have you nearby. But don't feel forced to stay. You may find that you're a more effective parent advocate if you get a good night's sleep in your own bed.
- **If you're not sleeping on site** but you're from out of town, that doesn't mean you have to pay a premium for hotels. Ronald McDonald House will accommodate families for a modest fee. There are a dozen across Canada. Some nearby hotels may even offer a discounted rate to parents of patients.
- **Always arrange** to be in the hospital room when the doctor is making his rounds. You'll get reports straight from the horse's mouth, and you'll have an opportunity to ask questions.
- **Nurses are people, too,** and they will respond to praise. Be sure to thank them for the great job they're doing. They'll be delighted to deal with you, and more likely to help you solve problems and get answers.
- **Don't forget to take time off.** If you need a few hours or a day to recharge your own batteries, send your spouse or a relative in your place.

Get in Touch

Children's Hospital of Eastern Ontario (CHEO) Virtual Tour
www.cheo.on.ca/virtual_tour

Ronald McDonald House Charities
1-800-387-8808
rmhc@ca.mcd.com
www.rmhc.ca

Pearl from a Parent
"The best thing I did was to make a booklet about my children to tell people briefly and in simple terms what they had, what they needed, and how others could help. When the kids were hospitalized, the nurses loved it because they knew what their needs were."

Meet the Meds Head-On

Whether it's liquids, pills, or chewable tablets, medications are a necessary part of everyday life for some children. In fact, over 40 per cent of kids with disabilities take prescription medication daily. As already mentioned, it's important to keep an up-to-date list of your little one's meds. Here are a few other tips:

- **Be clear about the purpose** of each medication your child is taking. If you aren't sure, don't feel foolish about double-checking with the doctor. He will likely be glad you spoke up.
- **Dispense medications** to your child in a quiet place with a calm manner.
- **Teach your child** to swallow pills by practising with a cake sprinkle.

Show her how you place it on the back of your own tongue and wash it down with a drink of water.

- **Give verbal praise** and even a small treat like a sticker to reward your child after taking medication.
- **Some pills** can be broken or crushed to make them easier to swallow, or even mixed with food like applesauce. Check with your child's health care provider or pharmacist to find out if this is possible.
- **If you do mix meds with munchies,** be upfront about it. Never try to trick your kid into swallowing his medicine. He'll only learn to distrust you (and hate applesauce!).
- **Many doctors** will routinely ask if your child is taking the proper dosage of his medication at the right times. If you aren't asked, do volunteer this information, because it's important. And be honest! Some children simply can't swallow pills, or won't accept a liquid without half of it ending up on her bib, and the doctor may have other options or ideas.

Treatment—What's the Alternative?

Moms and dads are often tempted by alternative therapies that promise spectacular results for their children. Sometimes parents turn to these treatments out of desperation. After all, you want the best for your kids. But the options can be overwhelming: vitamins, special diets, hyperbaric oxygen treatments, chelation therapy, hormones, acupuncture… Some remedies may help your child, while others may actually pose a risk of harm. How do you decide?

- **Don't assume** a supplement is safe because it's natural. All treatments can carry risk and cause side effects.
- **Keep your kid's doctor in the loop.** Let her know what treatments you are interested in trying and give her an opportunity to provide guidance.

- **If you are** signing your child up for therapies such as acupuncture or chiropractic, screen the practitioner as carefully as you would a primary health care provider.
- **Don't believe** everything you read on the Internet. Some health sites are reliable sources of information, but many are not.
- **Don't rely** on personal anecdotes for evidence. Learn about scientific trials, peer reviews, and how to interpret research results. And don't put stock in something just because you read about it in the news. A news story is often only a short summary of a complex study, and it may be open to interpretation.
- **Be wary of miracle cures.** If a tincture could really cure autism or asthma, wouldn't your pediatrician have proffered it by now?
- **Likewise, keep a tight hold** on your hard-earned dollars. Of course you'd pay anything to help your child, but it's money down the drain if the therapy is third-rate. As part of your research, get a range of perspectives, including one from a medical practitioner and one from an unbiased non-profit or watchdog group if possible.
- **Some treatments may be covered** by family insurance plans. Check with yours.
- **Don't set yourself up for disappointment.** Be aware that what helps one child may not help yours.

Get in Touch

Canadian Pediatric Complementary and Alternative Medicine Network (PedCAM)
www.pedcam.ca

National Center for Complementary and Alternative Medicine (U.S.A.)
301-519-3153
info@nccam.nih.gov
www.nccam.nih.gov/health

Got Intervention Apprehension?

Feeding tubes, catheters, shunts, and pumps. Yikes! Sometimes, kids with certain health conditions or disabilities need serious-sounding medical interventions to help them thrive. Truth be told, it can be terrifying to see your tiny tot wrapped with wires or tangled up in tubing. Often, it's a temporary treatment until she's stronger or healthier. Here are some tips for getting through it:

- **Don't let your nerves rule the day.** Of course a gastrostomy tube sounds scary. But there's a reason why the doctor is recommending it for your child, so hear him out.
- **Learn what you can** about the treatment and possible complications. The more information you have, the less foreign—and frightening—this new territory will feel.
- **Ask to be put in touch** with other parents who've been down this path. A candid conversation with another mom and dad may help put you at ease.
- **If possible, have the surgery or procedure** done at a hospital or clinic with a track record in this treatment. You're more likely to encounter nurses who are knowledgeable and can help with questions or complications.
- **If they're offered, do jump at the opportunity** to attend workshops that teach parents about the procedure and connect you with resource people.

Keeping Your Kid in the Pink

All boys and girls need a well-balanced diet, a good night's sleep, and a fit body to stay healthy. But it becomes more challenging when your child has a physical condition, a communication disorder, or a cognitive disability. A boy with cerebral palsy may have muscle spasms that interfere with sleep. A kid with autism may give a thumbs-down to new food textures and tastes. A child with spina bifida may not be able to stay in shape by running around the playground. But there are many ways to guide your child to good health.

Twelve Tips for Eating

1. Make sure your child eats regularly from all the food groups. Use Canada's Food Guide for information and ideas.

2. Avoid foods that are high in fat, sugar, and salt, or that have been heavily processed. Fast food and prepackaged snacks are usually a no-no.

3. Kids have teeny tummies and need frequent snacks to keep them filled. Offer healthy choices like yogurt, whole-wheat crackers, or cut-up fruit.

4. Avoid pop or sweetened juices, which are packed with sugar and void of nutrients, and don't leave much stomach space for healthy eating. Let your little one satisfy her thirst with water or milk.

5. Introduce a new food in small amounts—over and over again. Often even picky eaters will accept a new food after many exposures. Let her see you enjoying the food.

6. Don't use food as a reward, don't bribe your child to take a bite, and don't punish him for picking at his food.

7. Let your child help with meal preparation. If she washes the fruit or tears the lettuce she's more likely to sample the results. The bonus: It's great for her fine motor skills!

8. As much as possible, have relaxed, positive meals together as a family.

9. If your child has a physical disability, make sure she's well positioned for chowing down. You may need to consult with an occupational therapist to find out how your child should be seated or supported while eating.

10. Don't rush! Give your tot as much time as she needs to eat. This is especially important if she's still working on her ability to feed herself.

11. Ask the doctor if you should be supplementing your son or daughter's diet with a children's chewable multivitamin.

12. Kids with special needs sometimes have food sensitivities. Especially when your child is young, introduce only one new food at a time and watch for signs of food allergy or intolerance, such as a rash around his mouth, sore tummy, or diarrhea.

Get in Touch

Canada's Food Guide
To order a free copy, call 1-800-O-CANADA (1-800-622-6232)
Read online at www.hc-sc.gc.ca/fn-an/
food-guide-aliment/index_e.html

Just Take a Bite: Easy, Effective Answers to Food Aversions and Eating Challenges!
By Lori Ernsperger and Tania Stegen-Hanson

I-Can't-Chew Cookbook: Delicious Soft Recipes for People with Chewing, Swallowing and Dry Mouth Disorders
By J. Randy Wilson

Twelve Tips for Sleeping

1. Kids with disabilities often have sleep disorders, which can affect the whole family. If you think your child isn't getting the quality or quantity of sleep he needs, it's important that you seek professional help to get it solved.

2. Have a regular bedtime routine. If your child knows there's always

a bath and a book before bed, she'll start to relax before she even hits the pillow.

3. If your child has a communication disorder, consider using pictures or symbols to get her familiar with the bedtime routine and what is expected of her.

4. Make sure the sleeping room is a comfortable temperature, dark or only dimly lit, and quiet. Consider clearing the bedroom of toys, which can be distracting.

5. We all need to feel safe before we can sleep. Check in with your child if you think he's feeling anxiety at bedtime.

6. Make sure your child isn't hungry or thirsty before bed.

7. If your child naps, consider cutting back. Too much daytime napping can interfere with nodding off at night.

8. If your child is physically uncomfortable at night, ask a physiotherapist about better sleeping positions or a change in mattress, or talk to the doctor about a pain reliever.

9. If you regularly turn your child in bed, help her (and you) stay in sleep mode during these midnight meetings by keeping the room dim and your voice soft.

10. Some medications can cause wakefulness as a side effect. If you suspect this is happening, talk to the doctor about alternatives.

11. Keep a sleep diary. Record when your wee one falls asleep, how frequently she wakes up, and what happens during the wakeups. You'll have a useful record to share with the doctor.

12. If the specialist's strategies aren't working, go back and say so. Solving the sleep problems may require some trial and error. Don't give up. The health and well-being of your whole family is at stake.

Get in Touch

Paediatric Sleep Services
Alberta Children's Hospital
Calgary, Alberta
403-955-7563
www.calgaryhealthregion.ca/ACH

Sleep Better! A Guide to Improving Sleep for Children with Special Needs
By V. Mark Durand

Twelve Tips for Keeping Fit

1. Be active alongside your kid. Your support will help her participate more fully, and you'll also be setting a fine fitness example.

2. Make fitness fun. Let your kid build (or direct) an obstacle course that the whole family has to hustle over. Challenge your child to see how far he can stretch. Which toy can he reach?

3. There may be many activities in which your child has difficulty participating, but you can focus on one or two specific areas where she can develop a skill and feel proud. Teach her to swim like a fish, or help her learn to catch a curveball.

4. Think outside the box. Basketball hoops can be lowered for children without much strength or coordination. For playing catch, beanbags are easier to handle than baseballs.

5. Let your little one go at her own pace. Don't push her.

6. Play down the importance of winning. Focus instead on what your child is learning to do.

7. Check out your neighbourhood. Many community centres have accessible facilities, like swimming pools with lifts. Some bowling alleys have special ramps to help kids in wheelchairs launch a ball. When in doubt, ask about accommodations.

8. Specialty summer camps can accommodate kids with a range of

special needs like blindness, learning disabilities, or cerebral palsy while introducing them to swimming, canoeing, or hiking.

9. Be picky about fitness program leaders. Make sure they're positive and patient with your child. You don't want it to turn into a negative experience.

10. Use music. Kids of all ages and abilities have fun dancing or moving creatively to upbeat tunes.

11. If your child isn't very mobile, make a point of shifting her position every hour, and give her plenty of time out of her wheelchair.

12. The new Children's Fitness Tax Credit gives parents a tax credit for the money they spend on programs like dance or swimming lessons. If your child has a disability, you may be eligible for an additional $500 credit. So shell out! See Chapter 9 for more info.

Get in Touch

Active Living Alliance for Canadians with a Disability
1-800-771-0663
info@ala.ca
www.ala.ca

Camp Awakening
Provides an outdoor camping experience to children with disabilities.
416-487-8400
info@campawakening.com
www.campawakening.com

Canadian Therapeutic Riding Association
Lists horseback riding programs across Canada for children and adults with disabilities.
519-767-0700
ctra@golden.net
www.cantra.ca

Yoga for the Special Child: A Therapeutic Approach for Infants and Children with Down Syndrome, Cerebral Palsy and Learning Disabilities
By Sonia Sumar

General Resources For Health

Organizations

Canadian Institute of Child Health
613-230-8838
cich@cich.ca
www.cich.ca

CanChild Centre for Childhood Disability Research
McMaster University
905-525-9140, ext. 27850
canchild@mcmaster.ca
www.canchild.ca

Web

Canadian Health Network
www.canadian-health-network.ca

Caring for Kids
Canadian Paediatric Society
www.caringforkids.cps.ca

About Kids Health
The Hospital for Sick Children
www.aboutkidshealth.ca

"Pain, Pain, Go Away: Helping Children with Pain"
By Patrick J. McGrath, G. Allen Finley, and Judith Ritchie
Izaak Walton Killam Children's Hospital and Dalhousie
University
Read online at www.pediatric-pain.ca/ppga/ppga.html

"Tipsheet for Reducing and Managing Children's Stress"
Bloorview Kids Rehab
Read online at www.bloorview.ca/resourcecentre/
familyresources/managingkidsstress.php

Books

*Optimizing Care for Young Children with Special Health Care
Needs: Knowledge and Strategies for Navigating the System*
Edited by Elisa J. Sobo and Paul S. Kurtin

*When Your Child Has a Disability: The Complete Sourcebook of
Daily and Medical Care*
By Mark L. Batshaw

Navigating the School System

5

Meet Cole Robinson-Boivin
Whitehorse, Yukon

Had Cole Robinson-Boivin and his classmates been born two or three decades earlier, they probably never would have met each other. Cole wouldn't be learning algebra or science alongside twenty kids his own age. He wouldn't be chomping sandwiches with his circle of friends at lunch hour. He wouldn't be hanging out with his buddies at recess.

Thirty years ago, kids with autism weren't invited to attend public school with the other kids in their neighbourhood. But Cole has been part of his community school since day one. And when this grade twelve student graduates with a high-school diploma, he'll have the qualifications he needs to pursue post-secondary education. That's something he might never have had a chance to achieve in a segregated school.

"Cole really, really loves to study," says his mom, Julie Robinson. "That thirst for knowledge is one of his greatest strengths." He is particularly interested in biology, and his marks have earned him a regular spot on the school's honour list.

Despite his success, not every school has been prepared to welcome Cole with open arms. His family, who moved to Whitehorse from Kelowna, B.C., seven years ago, has been up against administrators who wanted Cole placed in a segregated class, teachers who didn't welcome Julie into the classroom, and principals who flatly said they couldn't meet Cole's high needs.

"There have been as many problems as joys," says Julie. "I've met people whose core belief is that children with disabilities slow the education process down." Thankfully, not everyone subscribed to this myth—including one particularly understanding school principal in Whitehorse who encouraged Cole to join his school and offered to supply an educational assistant. (Turned out his daughter has autism, too.)

Cole's educational assistant has now been in the classroom with him since grade five. She helps Cole manage his communication difficulties, sensory challenges, and coping behaviours. Julie says she deserves a lot of credit for how well Cole has done. "She's been riding the waves alongside him. She's as devoted to him as our family is."

Julie also counts her family lucky for moving to Whitehorse when they did. She's convinced it's been better for Cole. "The isolation influences the way of life here," she says. "Collective living, helping each other—it's really a strong part of the culture." And she points out that it's easier to lobby the government for positive change in a place where your MLA could be living right next door. "You have close proximity to the political system here." For instance, she and other parents have successfully pushed the territory's Ministry of Health to offer improved autism supports and services to Yukon families.

It's all about belonging. "Cole's inclusion in a typical class means that he's a member of the community in a fuller way than he would be in a segregated system," Julie notes. "People know him. He's downtown at the Superstore and people say, 'Hi, Cole, how are you doing?'" In a small town like Whitehorse, she says, that will almost certainly impact his employability. "That's one of the main ways people here get jobs—we know people."

And what does Cole's dream job look like? "He wants to go into animal science," says his mom. When Cole was just a toddler, he used to spend hours with his aunt's horses. Today, he loves bonding with his dog Comet. "When he's beside an animal, he is totally one with them. It's a moment of autism that is powerful," says Julie. "It's fascinating and beautiful to see."

Starting school is a rite of passage. Every parent remembers that fretful first day when she delivers her little darling into the (hopefully) capable hands of a smiling preschool teacher. When you're the parent of a child with a disability, it can be even more nerve-wracking. But who says you have to sit on the sidelines? Get involved! Be prepared to partner with your child's teacher and school, and you'll go a long way toward ensuring the best possible education outcome.

Give Me the Stats, Stat!

Are Canadian kids with special needs getting the education they're entitled to? The short answer is, sort of. Although more children with disabilities than ever—the vast majority of them, in fact—are being welcomed into regular neighbourhood schools, many aren't finding their needs fully met. Most of the time, say their parents, the stumbling blocks are lack of support staff, insufficient services, or out-of-reach assessments. And depending on a child's disability, or whether he attends school in an urban setting or a rural area, or even whether a child is a boy or a girl, there are often wide discrepancies in the level of services and support these kids are getting.

Yet experts agree that whopping changes in special education have taken place since the 1980s, especially in the past five years. Twenty years ago, kids with disabilities were often shut out of mainstream schools. Now, it seems, the system is in flux—but often still behind the eight ball when it comes to funding and staffing. All the more reason to do what you can to be an involved parent.

Signing Up for School

What kind of school setting is best for your child? There are different avenues for learning the three Rs.

- **Mainstream schools**

  Most kids with disabilities attend regular schools with children who have no special needs. Most take all the same classes as the other kids. The others are in resource classes for part or all of the day.

  Bonus points: Your child goes to school in her own community. For more information, see "Inclusion is Good for Kids with Disabilities!" on page 99.

  Demerit points: Disability services may not be up to snuff. Your child may not be automatically assigned an aide, even if you (and the teacher) feel she needs one. The school you want may not seem eager to accommodate your kid.

- **Therapeutic schools**

  A small number of kids with disabilities attend therapeutic schools, or "special schools," set up specifically for students with special needs.

  Bonus points: Your child has access to specialized supports and experienced teaching staff. Classes are generally small and staffing ratios high.

Demerit points: Your child will likely attend school outside of her neighbourhood and may face long days on a bus. She'll be in a segregated setting with less opportunity to socialize with non-disabled kids.

- **Homeschooling**
  Only a few kids with disabilities are schooled at home. But the number of homeschooled students across Canada in general has been rising.
  Bonus points: Your child receives an education program that is perfectly tailored to his abilities, and he moves at his own pace.
  Demerit points: Your child may miss out on certain therapies and supports that are traditionally offered through the public school system. He'll also spend less time with pals.

Pointers for Picking

So you want a mainstream school, but you're still wondering *where* to sign up your sweetie? Shop around! You may have more options than you think. Many Canadian communities have public schools, separate schools, *and* private schools close by. Here are some tips before you commit:

- **Know what you want.** What are your education goals for your child? Do you want her on the fast track to become a nuclear physicist, or do you just want her to make a few friends?
- **Be chatty.** Talk to the principal, vice-principal, and teacher…anyone who can offer insight into school policies and successes.
- **Check credentials.** Ask the principal if he has any special ed training. Ask him how he promotes inclusion in his classrooms.
- **Read between the lines.** A policy on paper is one thing. An

open-minded attitude is another thing entirely. Do the school staffers seem positive and upbeat about including your kid? Watch their body language.

- **Ask for concrete examples.** Are there other students with special needs like your child's? How are they being accommodated?
- **Get a feel for the culture.** Are there school activities to celebrate diversity? Are the hallways filled with artwork? Do staff seem inviting?
- **Trust your gut.** What are your instincts telling you?
- **Watch for a shift.** Sometimes a change in principal means a change in attitude. So if you have your heart set on the neighbourhood school—but the administration has put you off—check in again next year.

All about Inclusion

What is inclusion? It's been referred to a couple of times already in this chapter. Inclusion is an approach that is welcoming of everyone—with or without disabilities. Inclusive education means that kids with special needs are warmly included in neighbourhood schools, in regular classrooms, with kids their own age. It means they are given the accommodations and supports they need to participate in all aspects of their schools.

It may sound like a dream come true. But inclusion is something you have a right to advocate for and expect for your child.

That doesn't mean every school and classroom you come across will have arms wide open. But keep pushing. Education in Canada has come a long way in the last few years and it's no longer acceptable to ship kids to "special schools" on the other side of town. We now know it's good for kids with *and* without disabilities to be educated together. Make inclusion *your* mantra!

Inclusion is Good for Kids with Disabilities!

- **It gives them** a sense of belonging and being valued in their own communities.
- **It helps them** develop age-appropriate social skills.
- **It gives them** an opportunity to contribute just like other kids.

Inclusion is Good for Kids without Disabilities!

- **It teaches them** to value and be comfortable with all types of people.
- **It gives them** a greater awareness of disability issues and rights.
- **It teaches them** to become more compassionate and sensitive toward others.

Get in Touch

SpeciaLink: The National Centre for Child Care Inclusion
1-866-902-6333
info@specialinkcanada.org
www.specialinkcanada.org

Canada's Community Inclusion Initiative
www.communityinclusion.ca

Marsha Forest Centre
416-658-5363
inclusionpress@inclusion.com
www.marshaforest.com

Paving the Way

Want a successful inclusion experience? Get all the kids on board!

The other students in your kid's class may have questions or concerns about your child's disability. But once they catch on to your kid's special qualities, they'll be sure to rally around him. Help the teacher find books and even worksheets that will help the class learn more about your child's needs. See Chapter 2 for more on how to deal with other kids' questions about disability. If you're concerned about managing or preventing bullying, check out Chapter 6.

Get in Touch
Kids' Quest on Disability and Health
www.cdc.gov/ncbddd/kids/kidhome.htm

Connecting Kids: Exploring Diversity Together
By Linda Hill

My Friend with Autism: A Coloring Book for Peers and Siblings
By Beverly Bishop

How Come You Walk Funny?
This video documents an integrated kindergarten program, showing the similarities between kids with and without disabilities.
Symmetree Media
Available from Parentbooks
1-800-209-9182
www.cdc.gov/ncbddd/kids/kidhome.htm

Intricate Minds: Understanding Classmates with Asperger Syndrome
Available from Coulter Video
336-794-0298
www.coultervideo.com

Preparing Your Little Prince to be a Pupil

Whether your child is beginning a school year, moving to a new class, or starting school for the very first time, it can often be a trying transition. Here are a few ideas to smooth the process:

- **If possible, give your child** a chance to see the school, visit the classroom, and meet the teacher before starting school. He'll have a better idea of what to expect, and it won't seem so daunting.
- **Start on new routines** ahead of time. If your nipper will need to get up early for school, gradually move to an earlier bedtime and wake time over a period of days or weeks. If you'll be walking to school together every day, start including a stroll in your morning routine.
- **Talk about school**—activities, routines, and expectations for behaviour. But don't overdo it. Don't start cramming lessons down your little one's throat.
- **Don't overwhelm your child** with your own emotions. It's normal for you to feel anxious or apprehensive, especially when your kid has special needs. But children often channel their parents' moods, so try to keep your feelings in check.
- **Consider arranging playdates** with neighbourhood children whom you know will be in the same class as your kid. Pinpoint the kids who come across as especially compassionate.
- **Be sure to equip** the new classroom with medications, extra clothes, and supplies that your child may need to have on hand.
- **Scale back** on medical appointments and extracurriculars while your child gets used to the new school setting.
- **Make sure** your child is getting enough rest and nutrition during the transition.
- **Check in** with your child at the end of every day. If she's verbal, ask her what she did or what she's learning.
- **Don't worry** if your child seems exhausted and out of sorts at

first. It takes time to adjust to change. But do pay attention if these behaviour changes continue past the first few weeks—especially if he says he doesn't want to go to school—because it may mean something's up.

Dealing with the Administration

Teachers, principals, superintendents, and school boards...they all carry weight, and they all make decisions that affect your kid's school career. But they'd also all agree that you, as a parent, are a vitally important partner in your child's education. Here's how to work positively with all levels of administration:

- **Teach the teacher.** Offer pamphlets, printouts, or books that you think will help him understand and work with your child.
- **Explain how your tyke talks.** If your child uses augmentative and alternative communication such as sign language or picture symbols, be sure to share the specifics with the teacher.
- **Keep the lines of communication open.** Find out the teacher's preferred communication mode. Some teachers like a notebook, others prefer email, and still others rely on phone calls.

- **Get into a groove early.** If you want to know how much homework help to give your kid, or how often your teacher wants to meet with you, get set at the start of the school year.
- **Practise approaching the principal.** She's a big player in your pint-sized pupil's school experience. If you get to know her, she'll be more likely to help, and you'll be more comfortable approaching her.
- **Issue important items in ink.** If you have major concerns, put them in writing, even if you'll be at a face-to-face meeting. That way your comments will be documented and will stay in your child's file.
- **Present proof.** Don't just say you're unhappy with the accommodations. Bring evidence, like the science test that your child failed because the Individual Education Plan was not followed. (Fast fact: An Individual Education Plan [IEP] or Individual Program Plan [IPP] is a written plan of action that's designed to meet your child's special needs and her educational goals.)
- **Keep copies.** Hold on to copies of all your correspondence so you can refer to them if necessary, and so they are never lost.
- **Give praise when appropriate.** Write letters to the principal with positive feedback when it's deserved. When it comes time for criticism, you'll be taken more seriously.
- **Avoid being adversarial.** If you get steamed quickly, you won't solve anything. Try to work together as a team.
- **Keep your end of the bargain.** If you've asked for a communication book (a written notebook or binder in which you and the teacher communicate daily about your child), use it. If you've asked for work to be sent home, review it.
- **Never say no to a meeting.** Meetings give administration and parents a chance to touch base. Showing up for every meeting shows you're involved and available when it comes to your kid's schooling.
- **Remember, you know your child best.** Try to head off small problems before they blow up into big ones. Don't be afraid to suggest solutions.

Get in Touch

Parent Consultant in Education Online Training Program
Online course in parent advocacy.
Learning Disabilities Association of Ontario
416-929-4311
www.ldao.ca

Five Key Messages the Teacher Wants You to Know

1. **Have faith.** Most teachers truly want what's best for your child.
2. **You're not in the classroom six hours a day.** The teacher is, and she's likely to have a better handle on what goes on all day.
3. **Got a beef?** Before you head for the principal or superintendent's office, give the teacher a chance to make things right.
4. **But don't shoot the messenger.** Keep in mind that teachers don't have total control over school funding and board regulations. Sometimes, even if a teacher knows what your child needs, her hands are tied. In those cases, be sure to advocate at the right level—you'll get more action.
5. **Give guidance if it's required.** A less experienced teacher may need help to know how to accommodate your child. That's not the same as refusing accommodation.

Gold Star Idea

Keep your kid's teacher in the loop. Major events—and even minor changes—on the home front can affect your child's behaviour and focus at school. It helps your teacher to know something's up. So whether a new baby is born, a relative is visiting, you're taking time off from work or you're having the kitchen renovated, let the teacher in on it. As a consequence, she'll be a better source of support for your sweetcake.

Dealing with a Dud

While most teaching staff likely want to support your child, occasionally you may suspect that a particular teacher is not a good match for your child. You may have heard from other parents that the teacher can't cope with students who have special needs. Perhaps he hasn't received enough training. Perhaps he isn't open-minded. Perhaps he's burnt out. If you have a good reason to believe that your child will be better off in a different class, you may want to approach the administration and make your wishes known. A few pitfalls to avoid:

- **Don't sit back** and resign yourself (and your kid!) to a crummy year. Speak up while there's still time!
- **Don't wait until June to take action.** Meet with the principal in April or early May, before classroom planning for next year has begun.
- **Don't make demands.** Calmly explain your concerns. Tell the principal, "I'd feel more comfortable if my child were not placed in this class."
- **Don't close your own mind.** If the principal won't make any promises, or if she assures you that the teacher is terrific, try to

keep an open mind. The principal knows the teacher better than you do. But do keep constant tabs on what goes on in class.

General Resources for School

Organizations

Canadian Council for Exceptional Children
1-888-232-7733
service@canadian.cec.sped.org
http://canada.cec.sped.org

Research Alliance for Children with Special Needs
519-685-8680
racsn@tvcc.on.ca
www.racsn.ca

Special Education Technology (SET) — B.C.
604-261-9450
www.setbc.org

Centre for Inclusive Education
519-661-2111, ext. 88619
ghowell@uwo.ca
www.edu.uwo.ca/Inclusive_Education

Web

Special Needs Ontario Window: Cultivating Canada's Inclusive Education Community
www.snow.utoronto.ca

Inclusive Education
www.inclusiveeducation.ca

Parent's Advocacy in the School
www.parentsadvocacy.com

Books

*Believe in My Child with Special Needs! Helping Children
Achieve their Potential in School*
By Mary A. Falvey

*You're Going to Love this Kid! Teaching Students with Autism
in the Inclusive Classroom*
By Paula Kluth

The Survival Guide for Kids with LD
By Gary Fisher and Rhoda Cummings

Film

Going to School
This documentary follows three American seventh-graders with
disabilities as they are accommodated at school.
Available from Richard Cohen Films (U.S.)
310-838-4385
www.richardcohenfilms.com

Social Life and Extracurricular Activities

6

Meet Connor Pincombe
Notre-Dame-de-l'Île-Perrot, Quebec

Eleven-year-old Connor Pincombe is a little boy who likes games. His favourites are chess, soccer, and basketball. In fact, his parents don't bat an eye when they hear a lot of banging and thumping coming from his room—that's just the sound of Connor taking shots at the basketball hoop mounted on his cupboard door.

Connor has a global developmental disability that affects him in several areas, like communication and fine motor skills. He's also had two open-heart surgeries to correct cardiac issues. But he's active and healthy, and is definitely here for a good time.

His parents, Stacey Purcell and Andrew Pincombe, make sure that at least part of playtime for Connor involves other kids. Hanging out with friends helps him hone his social skills. "Socially, we try to make him seem as 'normal' as possible," says Stacey.

How do they help? Often, it means giving their son pointers in social situations. "A lot of times he doesn't know how to start a conversation with people," Stacey says. "He might just walk up to you and look at you and wait for you to say something, because he's not sure what to say." Connor's parents help him get in the groove by making suggestions about what he might say in different situations.

They've also been signing Connor up every summer for a soccer league geared to kids with disabilities. "He loves that," says Stacey. "He keeps asking, 'Are we playing soccer this week?'"

Every year, says Stacey, she sees her son grow and expand his social horizons. Last year, when his classmates began asking for each other's telephone numbers, their enterprising teacher got consent from parents and sent each student home with a phone list. "When he came home he said, 'Can I call one of my friends?' But before he could call them, they were calling here!" Stacey recalls. "Sometimes you wonder how the conversation is going. But it's fun for him, because he's excited about being able to call his friends."

This from a child who didn't speak until he was four. "Now he doesn't stop talking," laughs his mom.

Connor attends a small class in a school for kids with disabilities. Because children are kept in the same groups from year to year, it means he knows his classmates well by now. That comfort level helps when it comes to social time. His best friend, who attends the school with him, comes to play often—sometimes every day.

Other kids occasionally have questions about Connor, says Stacey, like friends who come to play with his nine-year-old brother Riley. She doesn't mind giving them simple explanations. But she has less patience for probing parents. "Riley's friend's mother sort of played twenty questions with Riley. I was a bit disturbed by that," she says. "There's even been friends of the family who say, 'What's wrong with him?' Those are the people where you keep it short and sweet and keep on moving." She admits that her family tends to avoid events where her son might be unfairly scrutinized. "We don't put ourselves in social situations that aren't comfortable for us as a family."

That doesn't mean they aren't out there, and having fun, too. They just choose their outlets—like the annual end-of-school party that has become legend at Connor's school, and where he always has a blast.

"We do everything we want to," says Stacey. "We don't stop because we have Connor."

For a variety of reasons, children with disabilities often have social strikes against them. Statistically, they are less likely than other kids to have a large network of friends, to feel included, and to feel liked. But these differences aren't usually huge, and they can often be overcome.

Since your child's early social development can shape the rest of his life, it's well worth investing time and focus on developing his social skills and enlisting him in social opportunities.

The Stumbling Blocks to Social Skills

It's true, lots of kids with disabilities will easily win the popularity vote with their playmates. But there are other kids with special needs who lag a little behind when it comes to developing social skills. There are many possible reasons for this:

- **Some conditions,** such as autism or learning disabilities, can interfere with reading body language, making eye contact, and figuring out how someone is feeling.
- **Disabilities like cerebral palsy and apraxia** can affect communication. Making friends is often more challenging for a kid who can't chat up her playmates.
- **Kids who aren't able to participate** fully in programs or schools because of a lack of accommodation are likely to have less practice with peers.
- **A disability can** also take away from social time if it means your child spends part of his day dealing with physiotherapy, tube feeding, or a lengthy bowel routine.

- **At recess,** classmates may exclude a kid with cognitive disabilities because they believe she won't understand the rules of the game they want to play.
- **Parents who feel** uneasy or intimidated by your child's special needs may hesitate to call for a playdate.
- **Kids with disabilities** themselves might hold back from bonding with buddies because of low self-confidence or self-esteem.
- **Children who** deal with lots of medical professionals are, let's face it, sometimes accustomed to being the centre of attention. It takes practice to learn to show interest in others.

Any of these challenges may mean your child is slower to develop some of the subtleties of social interactions like taking turns in conversation, sharing, smiling, or giving others their personal space. And they may exhibit inappropriate behaviour, such as talking too loudly, interrupting, acting bossy, or taking a classmates' crayons without asking.

What You Can Do

There are lots of ways you can help your honey hone those social skills.

- **Sign him up for social time.** Make a point of sourcing out schools and programs that are inclusive (accessible and accommodating), so your child will be welcomed to participate.
- **Do some people-watching.** Bring your child to public places where there will be adults and children, like stores and playgrounds. He'll have the chance to interact with other people, but he'll also have an opportunity to observe social behaviours.
- **Point things out.** Draw attention to what others are doing appropriately. Say, "See how that girl is looking right at the store clerk when she speaks to him? See how the children are waiting their turn on the slide?"

- **Practise at home.** Pretend you're the same age and try some role-playing. Pick scenarios like: "I have a new toy and you'd like to play with it," or "you'd like to trade snacks with me." If your child isn't sure what to say, write it down for her or rehearse it first.
- **Facilitate interactions.** If your kid wants to talk to another child but doesn't know how to start, you can initiate it by saying, "My daughter wants to ask you a question." Then help your child by prompting her: "Go ahead and tell Alana what you wanted to say."
- **Make a playdate with Destiny**—or Tiffany or Jessica or Kimberly. Ask your child's teacher to recommend a student in the class who is particularly compassionate, friendly, and popular. Then, invite her to a playdate she won't soon forget: Special snacks and fun-filled activities will keep her coming back.
- **Help your child with hygiene.** Other children don't want to play with a dirty, stinky kid. Make sure your child's hair, face, and hands are washed regularly, and dress him in clean, unstained clothes.
- **Help children choose sides with sensitivity.** If kids are being divvied into teams, use methods that won't exclude the less popular or coordinated kids. Sort them instead using questions like, "Who has a pet?" "Who has a birthday in the summertime?"
- **Nix the negative.** Explain why certain behaviours are inappropriate. Say, "Friends don't like it when you interrupt because it makes it seem as though you don't care what they're saying." If your child has odd habits like hand-flapping, encourage him to replace them with less noticeable behaviours like crossing his arms and squeezing tight under his armpits.
- **Praise the positive.** When your child tries to initiate social contact on her own, let her know how awesome she is! Tell her how much you'd like to see her do that again.
- **Get the in-laws on side.** Enlist the help of grandparents, aunts and uncles, even older siblings or cousins. Let them know that you've been reminding your child to use manners or speak softly.

Remember, don't go soft because of your child's special needs. If it's not okay for his sister to stay silent when the next-door neighbour says hello, then your son shouldn't be allowed to ignore him either. Expect the same etiquette from your child with disabilities. Don't be tempted to let the standards slip—you won't be doing him any favours in the long term.

Pearl from a Parent

"I give my daughter many reminders to always sign 'please' and 'thank you' to adults and children. She will do these without prompting now quite often. She catches on to naughty habits fast enough, so there is no reason why good social skills cannot be learned as well!"

Get in Touch

Social Skills Activities for Special Children
By Darlene Mannix

The New Social Story Book: Teaching Social Skills to Children and Adults with Autism, Asperger's Syndrome, and Other Autism Spectrum Disorders
By Carol Gray

Social Skills Training: For Children and Adolescents with Asperger Syndrome and Social-Communication Problems
By Jed Baker

Social Development Programs / Social Skills Programs
These programs teach specific social skills to children through activities and discussions.
Offered by the various chapters of the Learning Disabilities Association of Canada.

Call 613-238-5721 for your local chapter
www.ldac-taac.ca

"How to Develop Your Child's Social Skills"
By Sharon Lee
Read online at www.aqeta.qc.ca/article/sept05/sept05e.pdf

Bullying

Research has shown that children with disabilities are more likely to be bullied or teased than their peers without special needs. Does that mean your child is guaranteed to be victimized by her classmates? Not at all. But it's a good idea to be aware of the danger signs, and how to lower the bullying risk.

- **Keep the lines of communication open.** Talk to your child often about what's happening at school. You may find yourself bored silly by long stories about who wore new jeans or who was chosen for whose science partner. But if your child is accustomed to dishing about her day, she'll be more apt to speak up when it's something you'll want to know.
- **Work on your child's self-esteem** (see the section later in this chapter for tips). Kids with confidence are less likely to be victimized.
- **Teach your child** to move away from bullies, and to stay close to adult supervision.
- **Set up a support circle** or buddy system at school, so that your child is spending positive social time with others.
- **Help your child** enjoy academic success by working with him and his teacher to set goals—and cheer for every milestone that's met.
- **Raise awareness** by sharing bullying resources and websites with the teacher and encouraging class discussions.

- **Keep an eye on the way the teacher treats your tot**. His attitude is a model for other kids in the class. If the teacher speaks negatively about the disability or singles out your child unnecessarily, it may be worthwhile making an approach or even switching classes.
- **Be aware that there are many forms of bullying**. Bullying can be physical, like shoving or hitting, or verbal, like calling a child names. But bullying can also be more subtle. A bully might simply reject a child, telling her, "You can't play with us because you talk funny."
- **Pay attention** to personality or behaviour changes in your child like mood swings, clinginess, sudden bedwetting, new stomachaches. Take notice if she is trying to avoid school.
- **Don't drag your feet** if it sounds like your child is being targeted. Take immediate action: Talk to her teacher.

Get in Touch

Bullying.org
Offers resources, information, and presentations on bullying prevention.
www.bullying.org

"The 'Are' Word: Helping Individuals with Intellectual Disabilities Deal with Bullying and Teasing"
By Dave Hingsburger
Booklet available from Parentbooks, 1-800-209-9182
www.parentbooks.ca

"Bullying among Children and Youth with Disabilities and Special Needs"
U.S. Department of Health and Human Services
Read online at www.stopbullying-now.hrsa.gov/HHS_PSA/pdfs/SBN_Tip_24.pdf

"Bullying, Teasing and Put Downs: What Victims Can Do"
Workshop offered by the Montreal chapter of the Learning
Disabilities Association of Quebec
Contact Linda Aber
514-487-3533
tacticsmtl@yahoo.com

What If Your Kid's the Bully?

Children can bully for a variety of reasons. Sometimes they're unhappy, uncertain, or stressed. They may have been treated badly themselves. Perhaps they're seeking a feeling of power. They may not understand how their behaviour hurts others.

- **If you're told your child is bullying,** ask questions. Talk to peers, parents, or teachers. Find out when, where, and why the behaviour is happening. It may be true that your child—who is frustrated or unable to communicate clearly—is acting out or being aggressive. But is she really trying to control or intimidate others?
- **Don't be in denial.** If it becomes obvious your child is behaving like a bully, don't ignore it or make excuses for him.
- **Be aware** that when you confront your kid about the bullying, she may cry and blame the other children. This doesn't mean that she hasn't done anything wrong.
- **Remember that bullying behaviour can be changed.** Your kid isn't destined to become a hardened street criminal—especially if you intervene now.
- **Explain to your child** how his behaviour hurts other kids. In other social situations, not just this one, talk to him about how other people may be feeling.
- **Encourage him to share,** or even do volunteer work. Let him look after a pet.

- **Keep an eye on the homefront.** Is your child learning bullying behaviour from a sibling, for instance?
- **Be a good role model.** Tame your temper and watch your voice volume.
- **Kids with strong social skills are less likely to be bullies.** Work on the strategies earlier in this chapter.

Other Discipline Tips

It can be challenging to discipline a child with special needs, especially if she has difficulty communicating or understanding. But that doesn't mean you should let things slide. The long-term pay-off is a whopper! Here are some tips:

- **Use positive discipline techniques** like verbal reprimands, "time outs," and logical consequences to guide her behaviour and teach her what's unacceptable. Help her grow into a likeable, responsible person.
- **Look and listen.** Don't be so quick to slap on the old "behaviour problem" label. Your kid may be grabbing at a cookie because it's the only way he knows how to say he wants another one. Teach him a developmentally appropriate way to ask, like pointing, or saying (or signing) "please."
- **There's a strong link between** what your child eats and how she behaves or feels. Give the junk the elbow. Keep sugary, fatty, and highly processed foods to a minimum. Feed her a well-balanced diet, and offer frequent healthy snacks to keep that tiny tummy from growling.
- **Make sure your wee one is well rested.** See Chapter 4 for sleep tips. Consider an afternoon nap. It may make a positive difference to his behaviour and attention span.
- **Consistency is key.** If you give your child a warning or two and she doesn't listen, always follow through with a consequence.

Otherwise, she'll learn you don't really mean it.

- **Some learning disabilities make it harder** to get a child's attention. Instead of telling him to pick up his toys while he's engrossed in his action figures, touch his shoulder and make eye contact first.
- **Some cognitive disabilities may make it harder** for your child to learn the rules. Help her understand by breaking instructions down into simple language. Use repetition.
- **Depending on your child's developmental level,** he may not yet be ready for consequences. Use distraction and redirection to stop the behaviour you don't want, and keep forbidden fruit (like your antique glass collection) out of sight.
- **Never use humiliation to discipline your child.** You may try taking away activities like TV time, but don't take away essentials like medicine, meals, or security blankets. Avoid using physical punishment.
- **Remember that praise is discipline, too.** Give your kid positive feedback when he co-operates!

Tips for Raising Self-Esteem

The good news is there's no strong evidence to suggest that children with disabilities in general have lower self-esteem than other kids. But as we've already discussed, poor self-esteem can get in the way of forging friendships and it can even put your kid at risk for being bullied. If you think your child needs an ego boost, here are some ideas:

- **Praise goes plenty far.** But don't overdo it by telling your child that what she's done is fantastic when it's obvious to both of you that it isn't. On the other hand, sometimes it's appropriate to praise your child for making a good effort, even if she didn't get great results.
- **When your child fails at something,** help him keep it in

perspective. If he says, "I can never do anything right," remind him of what he does well, and that this is just one small setback.

- **When setting goals for your child,** make sure they're realistic so you're not also setting her up for failure.
- **Don't complain or speak negatively** about your kid's special needs when he's within earshot.
- **Assign chores to your child that are within** her abilities so she feels like a valued member of the household. If she is limited by what she can do physically, give her responsibilities like telling you when the kettle comes to a boil or making sure her younger sibling stays in his toddler bed.
- **Make sure** your little buddy's bookshelf includes stories that portray strong, confident characters with disabilities. Let him see that kids like him are a normal and important part of the community.
- **Similarly, if your child uses a wheelchair or hearing aids,** buy toys and dolls that also use these aids. The Little People Lil' Movers School Bus by Fisher Price comes with a wheelchair, for example.
- **Help your child link** to online peer support through websites set up especially for kids with special needs.
- **Play games, chat, or read with your child.** Cuddle him and stroke his hair. This lets him know that he's loveable and worth spending time with.

One final tip: Don't assume your kid is down on himself just because he's different. Pay attention to how he's really feeling—his self-esteem may be higher than you think. He may not care how he comes across to others, or he may not feel the need for scores of friends. If he's happy with who he is, then you should be, too. Just relax and enjoy your special little sprout.

Gold Star Idea

Think of ways to pump up your child's self-image. Help her choose trendy clothes or take her for a flattering haircut. If she uses assistive devices, try to make them fun and fashionable: Perhaps a bubblegum-pink wheelchair will reflect her bubbly personality. If she can't control her drooling, use a funky bandana to catch the drips instead of a babyish bib.

Get in Touch
Zoom!
By Robert Munsch

Seal Surfer
By Michael Foreman

Do Bananas Chew Gum?
By Jamie Gilson

Nobody Knows!
By Sarah Yates
Available from Gemma B. Publishing: 204-452-7566
www.gemmab.ca

Extraordinary People with Disabilities
Inspiring stories about forty-eight famous people with disabilities.
By Deborah Kent and Kathryn A. Quinlan

Multicultural Kids Inc. (U.S.)
Click on "Different Ability" to order dolls with visible disabilities.
1-877-686-7357
www.multiculturalkids.com

Ability Online
An Internet community connecting children and youth who
have disabilities and illnesses.
www.abilityonline.org

Party Central

Cake, ice cream, presents…who doesn't like a birthday party? (Well, maybe the parent who has to pull it off for twenty loud and sugar-high little tykes!) Whether your child is a guest or a guest of honour, consider these tips for success.

When Your Child Is Attending a Party

- **Talk to your child** ahead of time about what sort of activities and events are likely to happen at the party. This way, he'll remember what is expected of him and won't be overwhelmed by the unforeseen.
- **If your youngster** needs extra help to participate fully, ask the hosting mom ahead of time if you can stay for the party. Chances are she'll appreciate a spare set of hands when it's time to pass out cake and prizes.
- **What if your child** doesn't get invited to many parties? Use the money you save on gifts to buy an extra-special birthday present for the friend who does include your kid on the guest list.
- **Want to nurture a blossoming friendship?** Consider giving birthday gifts that will mean more social time spent with your child: movie passes for two, for example.

When Your Child Is Having a Party

- **Beforehand, give your kid** a primer on party etiquette: Greet every guest who arrives, say thank you when you open a gift.

- **Consider** putting a ceiling on the servings of sugary foods, which can aggravate problem behaviour. Serve foods high in fibre (like carrot sticks and whole-wheat crackers) and protein (like tuna fish) to temper the effects of the cake and ice cream.
- **Plan party games** that are done co-operatively as a group, rather than pitting each guest against the others in competitive contests.
- **Plan activities** that make the most of your child's abilities. Musical chairs might be a challenge if your child is blind, but she's sure to kick butt at Pin the Tail on the Donkey.
- **Want to show a DVD?** Captioned and narrated movies can be watched by kids who are deaf or blind, right alongside kids who aren't.

Extra-Special Extracurricular Experiences

Whether it's day camp or T-ball, drama class or tai kwan do, extracurricular activities do a lot for your little one. They get her out, actively participating and visible in the community. They give her a chance to explore interests, express her creativity, or develop skills. They even provide her with a sense of well-being.

Above all, they give your child an opportunity to socialize with other kids, whether or not they have disabilities themselves. Many special friendships form at camp or in clubs. And research shows that children with disabilities who are happily enrolled in extracurricular activities are more likely to be happy adults.

As a parent, you play an important role in the level of your child's community participation. There are many options, from sports to arts to music to outdoor recreation. They're offered by local community centres or sports complexes, disability organizations or municipal recreation departments, or as after-school programs. Many programs are accessible and accommodating, or can be with your intervention and ideas. So go ahead and sign on the dotted line!

Get in Touch

Canadian Therapeutic Riding Association (CanTRA)
519-767-0700
ctra@golden.net
www.cantra.ca

Active Living Alliance for Canadians with a Disability
Online resource tools for finding out more about adapted activities.
www.ala.ca/Content/Learning%20and%20Resources/
Overview.asp

Recreation Integration Victoria
Provides staff and assistance for children with disabilities attending recreational programs in this B.C. community.
250-477-6314
information@rivonline.org
www.rivonline.org

Sleepaway Camp

It may feel intimidating to send your sweetheart off to sleepaway camp, but many Canadian camps actually specialize in special needs. Disability-specific programs mean that counsellors will be better equipped to assist and even mentor your little one. And they teach your child that she isn't alone. These camps give your kid a chance to make friends, build skills and, often, learn more about managing her condition.

Get In Touch

"Your Kid Can Go To Summer Camp!"
Canadian Health Network
Read online at
www.canadian-health-network.ca

Easter Seals Camps
Runs twenty-two camps across Canada for kids with disabilities.
416-932-8382
info@easterseals.ca
www.easterseals.ca

Camp Awakening
Offers a sleepaway camping experience for Ontario children
with disabilities.
416-487-8400
info@campawakening.com
www.campawakening.com

Canadian Diabetes Association
Operates summer camps across Canada for kids with Type 1
diabetes.
1-800-BANTING
info@diabetes.ca
www.diabetes.ca/Section_services/camps.asp

Camp Freedom
An annual camping experience for western Canadian teens with
spina bifida.
Spina Bifida and Hydrocephalus Association of Northern
Alberta
780-451-6921
info@sbhana.org

CNIB Lake Joseph Centre
Offers recreational programs for Ontarians of all ages with
vision disabilities.
705-375-2630
lakejo@cnib.ca
www.cnib.ca/lakejo

General Resources for Social Life

Books

It's So Much Work to Be Your Friend: Helping the Child with Learning Disabilities Find Social Success
By Richard Lavoie

Families and Positive Behavior Support: Addressing Problem Behaviors in Family Contexts
By Joseph M. Lucyshyn, Glen Dunlap, and Richard W. Albin

Helping the Child Who Doesn't Fit In
By Stephen Nowicki Jr. and Marshall P. Duke

The Source® for Developmental Coordination Disorder (DCD)
By Paulene H. Kamps
Available from LinguiSystems: 1-800-776-4332
www.linguisystems.com

Family Relationships

7

Meet Kailyn Sneath
Spruce Grove, Alberta

Family gatherings at the Sneath house tend to be crowded and loud.

Not only does the clan include ten-year-old Kailyn, six-year-old Zachary, and new baby Julia, but virtually every other member of the extended Sneath family lives within an hour's drive of their home near Edmonton. So it's fair to say that family dynamics come into play often for the Sneaths.

"We have a good family life," mom Monica says. She and husband Del have long been accustomed to the special needs of Kailyn, who was born with spina bifida and has dealt with ongoing, often very serious, medical issues. They work around her tracheotomy and oxygen tank, her g-tube and catheters. And they focus on the fun.

Kailyn, after all, loves joking around. She likes playing board games. And she's hooked on speed. When her dad takes her for a ride on her grandpa's ATV, Kailyn is constantly urging him to go faster.

"There have been many times when we didn't think she was

going to make it," Monica says. "But you can't leave her in a bubble." Unfortunately, not every family member is as brave as she is about shedding the kid gloves. Both grandmas live nearby, but both have always been too terrified to take care of Kailyn on their own. A handful of well-meaning relatives even took a community course to learn how to manage Kailyn's medical issues—but have never had the nerve to actually pitch in.

"I know they've had a lot of guilt about not being able to help with Kailyn," says Monica. "My mom has been with me shopping and seen me resuscitate Kailyn in the middle of Baby Gap. That's stuck in her head. She never wants to be in that position."

But Monica points out that her extended family has been a wonderful support in other ways. For one thing, both grandmas willingly help with the other kids when needed. "As soon as Zachary came along, the babysitting door was wide open," says Monica. And that eases the stress when Kailyn has appointments or is in hospital. "You just don't want to be pushing a wheelchair and dragging along a newborn."

So what do the family dynamics look like within the Sneath walls? Kailyn gets along well with her little brother and sister, says mom. "Zachary and Kailyn have a very normal relationship. He helps her. They play together. But they fight over what movie they're going to watch or who has a turn on the computer, or he'll say, 'She's rolling over my toys!'" She notes that Zachary has taken on more of a big-brother role, but doesn't seem to notice the paradox. "It's all he's ever known. He's so comfortable with all of it."

And what about the bond between Mom and Dad? Monica and Del are convinced that having a child with a disability has only made their marriage stronger. "Any marriage has got the good, the bad, and the ugly," says Monica. "For the most part, things run smoothly. My husband and I have a good relationship."

Big-time travel bugs, the couple manages to get away together for a week every winter. (Kailyn can't travel, but last year Zachary tagged along.) "I've had friends and family say to me, I can't even imagine taking a family holiday and leaving one of your kids behind.

I say, you don't understand." In fact, a short vacation can be a shot in the arm for a mom and dad who face heavy-duty responsibilities at home. Thirteen successful years of marriage can't be wrong.

All in all, Monica asserts that family life is happy. "Our normal is a twisted sense of normal," she admits. "But that's been our life for years." And when she watches Kailyn crack up over a new joke, or grin from ear to ear as she zips along in her bike-powered chariot, this kind of normal seems pretty darn good.

When a child with a disability joins the family, all other members are affected, including parents, siblings, grandparents, aunts, and uncles. Some family relationships, such as your marriage or your ties to in-laws, may be sorely tested. Other relationships may be strengthened. This chapter will help you ride the highest waves of change—without falling headfirst into the surf.

Maintaining Your Marriage

Compared to the general population, the divorce rate is noticeably higher among couples who have kids with disabilities. Husbands and wives may be under added stress because of their child's special needs.

Then again, some couples report that the experience has made them a stronger, close-knit family. Either way, it can't hurt to review some ways to reduce the strain.

- **Find the time.** Set aside time in your day to talk, even if it's just five minutes by phone over the lunch hour. Next, schedule a regular day for spending a longer stretch of time together. Go for a drive or go for a coffee—it doesn't matter. What matters is that there are no distractions, and that it's just you and your date.
- **Talk about more than the kids.** That doesn't mean you need to

totally avoid the topic of children when you're together. But watch out—it's easy to slip into the habit of discussing nothing but the munchkins with your mate.

- **Keep the lines of communication open.** Try to be honest and open without incrimination. Encourage your partner to share his feelings, too.
- **Don't let problems fester.** If issues need to be cleared, better for your relationship that they are resolved quickly.
- **Be patient with each other.** Recognize that you have different coping methods, and that your communication skills may still be a work in progress.
- **Respect each other.** It's easy to allow a spouse to become a scapegoat. If you're feeling upset, annoyed, or like you're going off your gourd, do be candid about your feelings, but don't take it out on your partner.
- **Look for common ground.** Sometimes you and your partner might not agree on how to raise your child. You might not see eye to eye on behaviour management or medical interventions. What can help is learning everything you can, together, about the disability or treatment, or talking with professionals or experienced parents.
- **Don't discourage leisure time.** Playing sports, working on a hobby, or pursuing a special interest away from the rest of the family will help your spouse relax and refresh, and will in turn make him a better parent.
- **Don't forget to have fun.** Laughter is the best medicine. It won't cure your kid's condition, but it can help cement your relationship with your spouse.
- **Seek help if it's needed.** If your marriage is starting to show cracks and you're committed to saving it, consider counselling.

Consider Your Differences

Men and women often deal with problems in different ways. We also have individual differences in character that can affect how we cope. It may help you and your spouse to understand these differences, so you can be more sensitive to them.

Wives should try to understand that:

- Men often want to problem-solve. When they can't do anything about your child's epilepsy or asthma, they feel helpless and frustrated. This may come across to you as a negative vibe.
- If you are the primary caregiver (in almost all families, this will be the case), you may be feeling the pressure of your responsibilities. Do express what you're feeling. But don't cast blame. Focus on what you need, not on what he's not doing for you.
- If your husband spends much of the day at work, be aware that he may be feeling left out of your child's appointments, education, and development. He's also missing out on the support groups and social networks that are keeping you sane.

Husbands should try to understand that:

- Women get a lot of support through talking. You may have the urge to find a quick fix for every problem she comes to you with. But it may be that just by listening you will be helping her tremendously.

- If your wife is the primary caregiver, she may feel overwhelmed and underhelped. Consider whether you are contributing enough at home.
- Moms of children with disabilities are more likely to have health problems compared to other parents, including you. Encourage her to look after her own needs.

Get in Touch
Canadian Counselling Association
Find a marriage or couples counsellor in the website's online directory.
1-877-765-5565
info@ccacc.ca
www.ccacc.ca

Supporting the Sibs

Brothers and sisters of kids with special needs live a unique family experience. And while it's not all roses, these siblings often grow up to be strong, open-minded, and caring adults, and have a special bond with their brother or sister. Here's how to help them through.

Six Things to Remember about Siblings

1. Just like you, she may be dealing with feelings about having a family member with a disability. She may feel guilty, jealous, or embarrassed. She may worry or get scared. But she may hide her feelings from you. Teach her to express herself—it's healthy! Make sure she knows it's okay to share even when it's negative.
2. His milestones are important, too. He may not get as much

attention for learning to ride a bike as his brother does, but he may be just as proud of himself, so don't forget to cheer him on.

3. She needs to know the specifics about her sibling's special needs. You may think you're shielding her by downplaying the disability, but left to her own imagination, her fears (Is my sister going to die? Is she contagious?) may be grimmer than reality. Keep her in the loop, but keep the info age-appropriate.

4. He's not a caregiver or a nurse. It's fine to ask him to watch his little sister for a few minutes while you load the laundry machine. After all, you'd give him this job even if she didn't have a disability. But don't assign him too much responsibility for his sister's care. So where do you draw the line? He might think it's fun to feed his sister breakfast or put on her socks and shoes. But if it's seen as a chore, lay off.

5. She needs a break sometimes. She may love her big brother, but she thirsts for time apart, to be her own person. Arrange for her favourite aunt to take her to the zoo. Encourage her hobbies. Sign her up for extracurricular activities that don't include her sibling.

6. He's still a child. He craves your care, your attention, and your one-on-one time. When he's ignored, he may feel he isn't loved as much as his sibling with special needs.

Pearl from a Parent

"One of our largest difficulties is the guilt we feel over how much time we spend with our son versus our daughter. So often our daughter is dying for us to play with her, and it seems that there is either special food to prepare, or special homework sheets to prepare, or one-on-one time we need to spend with our son on whatever he needs to know. We often have to step back and remember how much she needs, too."

Family Relationships

Other quick tips for siblings

- **Link your child to peer support.** If you network with other parents of kids with disabilities, invite their non-disabled children for a playdate. Help your child access online listservs specifically for sibs. Read books about characters who have siblings with special needs.

- **Get a sitter.** If you are having trouble shoehorning in special time with your non-disabled child, hire a caregiver to watch his sibling while you take him to soccer. Make this your special night together, and go out for ice cream afterwards.

- **Play up her special privileges.** When it seems that the household revolves around her sib, help her remember the things that only she gets to do, like have a sleepover, ride her bike to the corner, or use the non-washable markers.

- **Don't blame the disability.** Don't tell him he has to miss the school picnic because of his sister's medical appointment. Instead of directly linking his disappointment with his sister's needs, explain that you simply have too many things to do that day. Better yet, arrange for the other parent or a relative to take him to the school event.

- **Don't say too much, too soon.** Although you should be open about the disability, there's no need to forecast the future while she's young. Of course, you're hoping she'll always be there to look out for her sister after you're gone, but don't lay this on her while she's little.

 Gold Star Idea

Want to give your non-disabled child some special mom-and-dad time, but can't get a sitter? Put your other kids to bed a little early, and keep him up a little late (if he's old enough). Then, break out the board games. Roll dice, jump squares, or deal cards—and enjoy the little conversations that crop up while you play together.

Get in Touch

The Sibling Support Project
www.siblingsupport.org

Ability Online
An Internet community connecting children and youth who have disabilities and illnesses, and their loved ones.
www.abilityonline.org

We'll Paint the Octopus Red
By Stephanie Stuve-Bodeen

And Don't Bring Jeremy
By Marilyn Levinson

Brotherly Feelings: Me, My Emotions and My Brother with Asperger's Syndrome
By Sam Frender and Robin Schiffmiller

"Supporting Siblings of Children with Disabilities"
Bloorview Kids Rehab
Read online at www.bloorview.ca/resourcecentre/
familyresources/siblingsanddisabilities.php

"How to Help Siblings of Children with Learning Disabilities"
Integra Resource Centre
Read online at
www.integra.on.ca

Living with a Brother or Sister with Special Needs: A Book for Sibs
By Donald Meyer and Patricia Vadasy

Siblings of Children with Autism: A Guide for Families
By Sandra Harris

"Brothers and Sisters"
A workshop offered to parents of children with disabilities in Vancouver, B.C.
Family Support Institute
1-800-441-5403

It's All Relative

Whew! If you initially thought a disability would only have an impact on your immediate family, you probably know by now that you were wrong. Your parents, siblings, cousins, uncles, aunts, and in-laws, or any combination thereof may all be affected by the birth of your baby. And as we all know, our extended kin can be a source of immense support, or utter annoyance.

What's Their Problem?

When it comes to your child with special needs, you may not always feel that your relatives understand. As you struggle to see eye to eye, it may be helpful to know what your relatives are thinking and feeling.

- **They may be overwhelmed** by feelings, just like the rest of your family. Grandpa may be grieving for the child he can never take camping. Your sister may feel guilty because her kids don't have disabilities.

- **Extended family members** can't read your mind, and they may not realize how exhausting and difficult your job is. If you want their support, be open about some of the responsibilities that keep you hopping.
- **When relatives** make critical comments about your parenting, it can make you feel incompetent and defensive. And it can also seem as though they're overly negative about your child's needs. But consider this: They'd probably be just as outspoken if your kids had no disabilities. That's part of the charm of an extended family.
- **If relatives** seem more willing to look after your children without disabilities, it may feel as though they're rejecting your child with special needs. But this doesn't mean they love her any less. Perhaps they are doubtful they can care for as well as you can. They may be intimidated by her extra needs. Offer to teach them how to use a catheter or say a few words in sign language.
- **Some of your relatives** aren't as enlightened as you are (or as you're quickly becoming) about disability issues. In Grandma's day, back in the mid-twentieth century, many people considered the birth of a child with a disability to be a disaster. These kids were institutionalized, or worse. Few, if any, of your older relatives grew up with classmates with special needs, and they simply have no idea of their potential.
- **Enlightened or not,** your extended family members still don't know the ins and outs of your child's needs as intimately as you do. So when they offer cake to your kid who's on a gluten-free diet, don't be so fast to fault them. Just correct them gently.

Hero Sandwich, Anyone?

Many moms and dads of kids with disabilities are also dealing with their own aging parents. Being a member of the sandwich generation is challenging enough for anyone because you're often balancing the needs of your frail folks with your demanding little dumplings. When one of your kids has special needs, there's even more on your shoulders. Here are some survival tactics:

- **Share the load.** Encourage your brothers and sisters to be involved with your elderly folks. Believe it or not, sometimes it's assumed that a family member who is already experienced in dealing with disability issues is a prime candidate to care for older parents.
- **Encourage bonding.** If your parents are too elderly to look after your child with special needs, or if they have arthritis, low vision, or hearing difficulties that interfere with picking him up or playing with him, they may need some extra encouragement to bond. Talk to them often about your child's interests and milestones. And tell your child special stories about Grandma and Grandpa, or have her draw them a picture of one of her favourite activities.
- **Respect energy levels.** Your child's daily demands or behaviour issues may be exhausting for your parents to be around. Keep visits short, so they remain a positive experience for everyone. If your parents live in another town, consider booking rooms at a nearby motel instead of bunking in with them.
- **Draw the line.** You can't do everything for everybody, so say no to what you're not able to handle. Don't be a hero sandwich. You're no good to anybody if you're burnt out. If that means your parent must be cared for in a facility, accept that fact and release the guilt if you can.

Single Parent Pointers

Parenting on your own? You're not alone. One in every five young kids with disabilities lives with a single parent. Although there can be emotional and financial disadvantages to raising a kid with special needs on your own, some single parents find they're able to devote more time to their children because they aren't focusing on maintaining a marriage as well.

Do remember, though, that if your ex is still in the picture it's critical that you keep cordial relations with him. Be polite, and don't argue or hurl insults. Respect each other's perspectives and share information freely about your child, so that it's easier to make major medical or treatment decisions jointly. Even though you're no longer living under the same roof, you're still a parenting team, and your child needs you to work well together. If you're having problems, seek counselling together to learn how to communicate effectively.

More to Keep in Mind

- **Your child may** blame himself or his disability for the break-up of his mom and dad. Make sure he understands that it is not his fault, and that you both love him as much as before.
- **Keep on the lookout** for self-esteem problems in your kid, which can crop up after parents split. See Chapter 6 for tips on boosting self-esteem.
- **Kids who are** coping with changes in the home may also show more behavioural difficulties. Speak to your child's doctor, therapist, or teacher as early as possible, before small problems become big ones.
- **If your child** spends time in two households, try to keep things as consistent as you can. The rules should be the same, if possible. Behaviour that is outlawed in your home should be just as unacceptable at your ex-spouse's place.
- **If you are the primary caregiver,** you may feel alone and unsupported. It's important that you look after yourself, not just your kids. They need you to be in top form. (See Chapter 8 for more on nurturing your needs.)
- **Children of single parents** are more than three times as likely

as other kids to live in a low-income situation. Disabilities often create a greater financial demand on the family. Look for ways to make the most of your money by following the tips in Chapter 9 of this book.

Get in Touch
50 Wonderful Ways to Be a Single-Parent Family
By Barry Ginsberg

Step-Parent Suggestions

Are you the step-parent of a child with a disability? Lucky him—if you're reading this book, then you're likely very involved and caring. And you play an important part in his life. Depending on the age of the child when you join the family, often you bring with you an outside perspective, shedding new light on particular disability issues that may have been challenging the family.

- **If his other biological parent is still in the picture,** it's important that you respect each other's roles. The natural parent may feel competitive or threatened by your participation in her son's life. But there's certainly room for all the parent figures to have a relationship with the child.
- **Don't hesitate to parent the child** with the same discipline and positive reinforcement that he receives from his biological parents. You'll form a better bond if you're involved with him, not distant.
- **Always speak of the biological parent with respect.** Try to be congenial in your contact with her. Remember, you'll be working together for a long time, and you all have the child's best interests at heart.

Get in Touch

The Stepmom's Guide to Simplifying Your Life
By Karon Phillips Goodman

Seven Steps to Bonding with Your Stepchild
By Suzen Ziegahn

The StepFamily Foundation of Alberta
403-245-5744
info@stepfamily.ca
www.stepfamily.ca

General Resources for Family Relationships

Organizations

Family Service Canada
Provides information and advocacy to strengthen families.
1-800-668-7808
info@familyservicecanada.org
www.familyservicecanada.org

Vanier Institute of the Family
Creates awareness of the importance of family, and promotes
the ability of families to help themselves.
613-228-8500
webmaster@vifamily.ca
www.vifamily.ca

Family Support Institute
Supports families in B.C. that have a member with a disability.
1-800-441-5403

fsi@bcacl.org
www.familysupportbc.com

Web

"Children with Disabilities and Their Families in Canada: A
Discussion Paper"
National Children's Alliance
Read online at www.nationalchildrensalliance.com

"Families Living with Disability"
Transition Magazine, Special Edition
Vanier Institute of the Family
Read online at www.vifamily.ca/library/transition/321/321.pdf

Film

One of the Family
Four families of children with special needs share their parenting values.
Available from Program Development Associates (U.S.)
1-800-543-2119

Outside the Domain
of Disability   8

Meet Gemma Yates-Howorth's Mom
Winnipeg, Manitoba

Sarah Yates-Howorth is a woman of many talents. She's an accomplished writer and lecturer. She's a disability advocate. She's a great mom.

But Sarah's single most important gift is probably her ability to recognize her own limits. The fact is, if she hadn't been blessed with this instinct, she almost certainly would have snapped years ago.

It would be so easy for someone else in Sarah's shoes to get snowed under. Her bright and artistic daughter, 19-year-old Gemma, has cerebral palsy. Her husband, Ted, also uses a wheelchair. Her mother was always too frail to offer physical help and her sisters live too far away.

But when Ted's aging parents came to live in Winnipeg to be closer to the family, that's when Sarah spoke up.

"I can't do any more caregiving," she recalls saying at the time.

Sarah's view is simple: If she breaks down, the family will follow.

So it's critical that she not take on more than she can handle. "I can't say I always do it without guilt," she admits. "But you have to become very tough." Instead, Sarah demonstrates her affection for her in-laws by inviting them to dinner and hiring an attendant to help out.

Sarah is scrupulous when it comes to finding time for herself. Her favoured escapes are writing and reading. "I never go to bed without reading. I can't imagine it," she says. And now that Gemma has developed into a book lover like her mom, the two often read aloud together, a pastime Sarah finds exceedingly relaxing.

She also stays on the move. Her daily meandering walks through Winnipeg keep her body toned ("I've seen too many big-bottomed women writers, and I'm too vain," she laughs), but they serve as an emotional outlet too. "When I walk, I can shout. I can dance. When I'm walking, my mind can unravel." She'll walk the shores of the Assiniboine River in all seasons, or hoof it to the store or a downtown meeting. Even when Gemma was little, Sarah would find a way to get out. "Sometimes I would be pushing her," she says, "but it would also be for me."

For years, Sarah has hired people to help with Gemma. And as Gemma has matured she has shared the management of these services, easing another duty off Mom's shoulders. Having extra hands around has been a boon. "It's given her time away from me, and me time away," Sarah says.

That doesn't mean Sarah hasn't had her moments off the rails. When her husband was having increasing difficulty walking but wasn't yet ready to use a wheelchair, her own responsibilities ramped up. "I nearly almost broke in half," she says. "I didn't get time out unless I fell over." What helped was, again, to know when to say no. Sarah also learned to link up with other moms who were raising kids with cerebral palsy and could understand a little of what she was going through. "They were wonderful," she says. "I think peer support is very important."

The occasional vacation doesn't hurt, either. Sarah relishes the trips she's shared over the years with her daughter, saying it has strengthened their bond. And she and Ted go out on dates to dinner or art galleries, sharing their passion for art and each other. "I've been lucky to have a husband who supports me and encourages me to pursue my own interests."

Sarah is proud of Gemma, who has grown into a sensitive, creative young woman. Gemma likes to write stories and draw, cook and sew, and scores good marks at school. She wants to become a designer—she's constantly redecorating her room. She clearly has a bright future ahead.

As a parent of a child with special needs, looking after yourself can be challenging. "I think it's always a balancing act," says Sarah. "But one thing's for sure—Gemma becomes daily a more interesting and insightful person. I wouldn't have traded her for the world."

Sometimes it seems like your world revolves around your children. But you have a life, and it's important that your needs are taken care of as well. As one parent puts it: "When Mom's not happy, no one's happy." A study shows that most parents who need extra support because of their child's disability, like time off or help with chores, rarely get it. This chapter, packed with ideas and resources, will help you zero in on you.

Fair warning: This chapter is admittedly mom-heavy. But that's because in the vast majority of families of children with disabilities, Mom is the main caregiver. If you're a dad, you're definitely not meant to be excluded from this chapter. Most of these tips will bolster you, too.

Looking after Yourself

Here's the bad news: If you're a mom of a child with special needs, you're half as likely to be healthy as all the other moms at school. No wonder they have the energy to make home brownies for the class bake sale while you just grabbed a pack of powdered doughnuts at the corner store. (Feel less guilty now?)

The fact is, being a mom or dad of a kid with disabilities can be draining. You have less time to yourself, and you end up focusing less on your own needs. But it's critical that you carve out me-time on a regular basis. If you think that's selfish, think again. You are a much more effective parent when you're in the pink.

It's not only your physical health that can suffer when you're constantly in demand. It's your emotional health, too. With that in mind, here are some tips for looking after your body *and* soul.

Body...

- **Get regular exercise.** That doesn't mean you have to commit to the gym for two hours every morning. But you can take the stairs, park farther from the store entrance, or dance like a dervish when your favourite song comes on the radio. It all adds up.
- **Eat well.** You'll have more energy highs and fewer sugar lows if you eat well-balanced meals and snacks instead of prepackaged foods high in carbs and sugars. Even when you're busy, a fresh apple is just as portable as a fat-packed muffin. Refer to Canada's Food Guide to find out more.
- **Get enough rest.** Don't sacrifice your sleep for anything. Sleep-deprived adults face more health risks—and we all know from experience how useless we feel when we're tired. Invest in a comfortable mattress, go to bed at the same time every night, and set aside eight straight hours for sleep.
- **Schedule regular checkups.** You should have a complete physical every year to 18 months, but it's easy to let it slip. Put a reminder in your calendar.
- **Take a shot.** Vaccinations are available that can guard against certain sicknesses that might otherwise sap your immune system.

Ask your doctor about flu, chicken pox, and pneumococcal innoculations.

- **Quit smoking** and ditch other unhealthy habits like too much drinking. Your body will thank you immediately.

...And Soul

- **Learn to relax.** Sit comfortably in a quiet place, breathe deeply, and systematically loosen the tension out of each of your muscles. Don't forget your shoulders, and the area around your eyes.
- **Pursue a hobby.** Spend time on an activity you enjoy, whether it's scrapbooking, painting, or cross-stitching. Work on your tennis serve. Develop your photographer's eye.
- **Connect with the great outdoors.** Go on a nature walk, breathe the clean air, and drink in the beauty around you. Meditate in the backyard and listen to the robins warble. Dig in the garden—research suggests the friendly bacteria in the soil may lift your spirits.
- **Be with friends.** Your time is precious, so pick the pals you have the most fun with—or the most deeply satisfying conversations.
- **Laugh it up.** Watch a funny movie, check out the comedy channel on TV, read side-splitting stories, or go through the Saturday comics.
- **Tap your inner divinity.** Not everyone has a spiritual side. But if you do, you may find peace through prayer or by getting in touch with your faith.

Get in Touch
Healthy Living Unit
Public Health Agency of Canada
www.phac-aspc.gc.ca/pau-uap/paguide/activities.html

"On the Road to Quitting: Guide to Becoming a Non-Smoker"
Health Canada
To order a free copy, call 1-800-635-7943
Read online at www.hc-sc.gc.ca

Canada's Food Guide
To order a free copy, call 1-800-O-CANADA (1-800-622-6232)
Read online at www.hc-sc.gc.ca/fn-an/
food-guide-aliment/index_e.html

Laughter Yoga
Join a laughter club in your community!
www.laughteryoga.ca

Canadian Women's Health Network
1-888-818-9172
www.cwhn.ca

When You're on the Edge

As richly rewarding as parenting can be, no one ever promised it was easy. Sometimes moms and dads of kids with special needs feel especially stressed. Here are some solutions for staving off a disaster.

- **Just say no.** Take careful stock of your commitments: Are you saying yes too often? No one wins if you're pulled in too many directions to follow through properly on your promises. Start putting a limit on what you agree to take on.
- **Do a reality check.** Are you expecting too much from others, only to be let down again and again? By setting your standards too high, you may be setting yourself up for constant disappointment.
- **Vent your feelings in a healthful way.** This can mean talking

to a counsellor or friend, going for a long run or writing in a journal.

- **Learn how to deal with frustration.** Take a course or read a self-help book on stress or anger management.

- **If you're feeling down, talk to your doctor.** If you often feel like crying, if you have difficulty concentrating, if you're easily agitated or you're sometimes asking yourself, "What's the point?", you may have depression. See your doctor right away—it's treatable, not hopeless.

- **If you think you'll abuse your kid, make a call.** If you feel like you can't cope, if your child's constant needs are making you feel angry or resentful towards her, if you're screaming things you regret, or you find yourself handling her too roughly, don't let it get out of hand. Contact your local Children's Aid Society for help. This doesn't mean your child will be taken away. The first priority of a child welfare society is to support you in being an effective parent.

Get in Touch

"Tipsheet for Reducing and Managing Stress"
Bloorview Kids Rehab
Read online at www.bloorview.ca/resourcecentre/
familyresources/managingstress.php

Don't Sweat the Small Stuff...And It's All Small Stuff
By Richard Carlson

Child Welfare League of Canada
613-235-4412
info@cwlc.ca
www.cwlc.ca

Ontario Association of Children's Aid Societies
416-987-7725
www.oacas.org

The Person Within: Preventing Abuse of Children and Young People with Disabilities
Video gives tips for safeguarding kids with disabilities against abuse and neglect.
Available from the BC Institute Against Family Violence
1-877-755-7055
www.bcifv.org

Give You a Break

You can't care for your kids around the clock. So who looks after them when you're off duty? Some parents turn to agencies that offer respite services. Often this is paid for by the provincial government. Others use ordinary babysitters with extraordinary training. Still others rely only on relatives.

Some moms and dads sign their youngsters up for day care. This can be a frustrating experience, as unaccommodating staff are sometimes quick to close their minds when they see your kid coming. But take heart: More and more Canadian child care centres are developing policies and training to be more inclusive of children with special needs. See Chapter 5 for more on inclusion.

Gold Star Idea

Good caregivers are gold. If you've managed to find a babysitter who is reliable, compassionate, and can handle your half-pint, do what you can to make sure she sticks around. Treat her with respect and kindness. Remember her with small gifts or cards on special occasions. Offer flexibility when she needs it. Don't skimp on her salary. And say thank you—no one ever gets tired of hearing it!

Get in Touch

Children with Special Needs
Ontario Ministry of Children and Youth Services
416-325-0500
www.children.gov.on.ca/mcys/english/programs/needs/index.asp

Family Support for Children with Disabilities
Alberta Children's Services
780-427-2551
www.child.alberta.ca/home/591.cfm

SpeciaLink: The National Centre for Child Care Inclusion
1-866-902-6333
info@specialinkcanada.org
www.specialinkcanada.org

Canadian Child Care Federation
613-729-5289
info@cccf-fcsge.ca
www.cccf-fcsge.ca

Pearls from a Posse of Parents

What do you do to focus on yourself? Here, eight moms of kids with special needs talk about what they do with their me-time. Read on, and get inspired with ideas!

"I take a pilates class twice a week and occasionally go to the gym. I love having no interruptions for an hour!"

"I like to read when the kids are in bed."

"If I feel the need to escape I will run to the mall, get a juice, and window shop. Sometimes I do the grocery shopping in the evening after bedtime. I will pick a smaller grocery store so I know it won't be busy."

"I like to put the music on loud and clean house. I think it's the freedom of going from room to room without someone stopping me and making me change direction—it is very liberating."

"When I start to feel topsy-turvy I know it is time to spend more time in prayer. I also attend a weekly Bible study group."

"I started boot camp. It takes place at a local gym, and we do circuits with weights and exercise equipment."

"Bubble baths are the fifteen-minute escape. Any longer, and the calls for 'mom' start. I definitely need bubbles, a special drink—and a book, because it's the only time to read."

Payday! Working Outside the Home

If you feel like your child's special needs are having an impact on your job (or lack of one), you're not alone. A Statistics Canada study showed that just over half of all parents who have children with disabilities feel that their employment situations are affected. Some moms and dads work fewer hours. Others change their work schedule to suit their children's needs.

Some give up employment altogether, electing to be stay-at-home parents. Yet for many moms and dads, quitting work is not an option. Perhaps you can't do without the income. Or perhaps you can't do without the change of pace, sense of identity, and satisfaction that your job gives you. Below are some strategies for making your job work.

Think Outside the Cubicle

Looking for that balance between drudgery and family? Here's what some working parents of kids with disabilities are doing to create solutions:

- **They telecommute.** Some or all of their work hours are spent at home. It cuts back on commuting time, and puts them in closer touch with family.
- **They flex their hours.** Have to leave early to take your tot to therapy? Not a problem, if you're at your desk an hour before everyone else in the morning.
- **They work part-time.** This allows them to plan around pediatric appointments and play groups without taking time off.
- **They job-share.** They work fewer hours but the job still gets done...because a compatible work partner picks up the slack while they're gone.

- **They become their own boss.** Consulting, contracting, or free-lancing allows them to accept work or turn it down as it fits their family's needs. Plus they can take an entire day off and then burn the midnight oil as they please.
- **They bring their offspring to the office.** Babies don't belong at every job site, but at some workplaces, employees have been known to tote along a tiny tyke in a playpen. Failing that, many corporations offer on-site daycare.
- **They work in the family business.** Okay, it's not an option open to everyone, but one thing is for sure: Your boss is a heck of a lot more understanding of your child's needs if we're talking precious granddaughter.
- **They take jobs in the non-profit sector.** Often, a disability organization or social agency, being in the business of helping people, is more open to offering flexibility for families.
- **They open up to their employer.** Sounds simple, right? A straightforward approach may score more points with your manager than a slew of furtive phone calls. Try saying, "My son has cerebral palsy, and sometimes his caregiver needs to call me. The days that I spend time on personal calls, I will take a shorter lunch."

Tips for Negotiating Flexibility at Work

- **Before you approach your boss, prepare a written proposal.** You can find templates online or make up your own. Try rehearsing your presentation with a trusted co-worker.
- **Do some legwork first.** Find statistics on productivity levels in companies that offer flexibility. Canvass your customers to find out how they'd feel if you were job-sharing, or available for different hours on different days.
- **Get well-versed on your company's policies.** They may be more supportive than you suspect.

- **Find out if other**s in your workplace have been allowed flexible hours, and whether or not it's been successful. Find out if your employer's competition offers flexibility to its workers.
- **Anticipate your boss's objections,** and have answers to her concerns at the ready. Is she worried you won't be accountable if you work odd hours? Offer to submit a regular report of your day's accomplishments.
- **It doesn't hurt** to remind your employer of your value to the organization. Highlight the qualities that would help you be productive under the proposed arrangements. For instance: "I work best without distraction, so I will be able to focus in my home office."
- **Suggest a trial period,** during which you can prove how well the new arrangement is working—or decide it's not for you after all.
- **Be patient.** Your employer may initially turn you down, or may struggle with a few sticking points. Talk to him again at a later date, presenting new solutions to address his concerns.

What Are Your Rights?

You may think your boss always has the last word, but the truth is you do have rights. The company you work for may have a written policy that supports working parents. For example, the Royal Bank of Canada offers dependent care support and flexible work arrangements. Plus, your provincial ministry of labour issues standards that employers must follow. Under Ontario's *Employment Standards Act*, for example, you may be eligible for personal emergency leave if your child has an illness or surgery. Under New Brunswick legislation, you may be permitted to take family responsibility leave to care for your kid in a pinch.

Get in Touch

Canadian Telework Association
613-692-0566
info@ivc.ca
www.ivc.ca

University of California at Berkeley
Telecommuting Proposal Template
http://hrweb.berkeley.edu/POLICY/teleppsl.htm

"Your Rights at Work"
Ontario Ministry of Labour
1-800-531-5551
Read online at
www.labour.gov.on.ca/english/es/brochures/br_rights.html

New Brunswick Employment Standards
1-888-452-2687
www.gnb.ca/0308/002e.htm

Work-Life Balance in Canadian Workplaces
Human Resources and Social Development Canada
www.hrsdc.gc.ca/en/gateways/topics/wnc-gxr.shtml

Family Work Connections
Lists Canadian resources such as websites, online articles, and
book titles.
www.cfc-efc.ca/family_work

Work Family Tips
www.wft-ifb.ca

Globetrotting! Travelling as a Family

Likely no parent needs a vacation more than you! But before you rush to pack your bags, consider these ideas for keeping a family trip from falling flat.

- **Do your research and take your time.** Make up a list of accommodation must-haves for your munchkin, whether it's running water or a hot tub, and use it as a checklist when you're speaking with a booking agent. Ask other parents of kids with special needs about their travel successes.
- **Call hotels directly.** If you need a wheelchair-accessible guestroom and want to know more details about the room size or washroom, forget about calling a reservations hotline. The booking agent who takes your call has probably never laid eyes on the hotel you're travelling to. Instead, put a direct call in to hotel management, or even the housekeeping department. Calling the hotel directly is also an opportunity to ask for other special accommodations.
- **Choose a well-known transportation company.** When it comes to accessibility and family-friendly service, you may be better off picking the most prominent air and bus lines. They have policies on special needs and are likely to score highest (although it's not a hard-and-fast rule).
- **Be outspoken about your child's needs.** When you make your hotel or airline reservation, make it clear what help you'll want. Do you need an escort to help your family through the airport? Will your child require a special meal? Now is the time to say so. But keep in mind that you may need to repeat your requests on the day you travel.
- **Talk to your child about what to expect.** Some kids with disabilities have difficulty with unfamiliar places or changes in routine. Have a chat with your child about where you're going and how you'll get there, and what it will be like.

- **Prepare for emergencies.** Take out travel insurance. Bring a written health summary of your child's disabilities, surgeries, and medications. Carry a photo and description of your child in case she wanders off.
- **Arrive at the station early.** Families with small children or those needing special assistance are often boarded onto trains or airplanes ahead of other passengers.
- **Need air? Be aware.** If your child uses supplemental oxygen, she probably won't be allowed to use her own tanks on the plane. Most airlines will supply oxygen for a fee.
- **Cram your carry-on.** Bring all your child's medications in your carry-on luggage, along with prescriptions. Store the medications in their original containers. Call the airline to find out what else you can—or can't—bring on board. Often, mobility devices like walkers or wheelchair cushions can come in the cabin without being counted as a piece of carry-on.
- **Stock up for the superhighway.** If you're travelling by car, make sure you're carrying a good supply of food, water, diapers, and medicine—anything you'll need if you have a car breakdown, or get stuck in the mother of all traffic jams.
- **Make your road trips fly by.** To reduce the number of times you hear "Are we there yet?", consider driving at naptime or bedtime, buying children's audiobooks, or renting a portable DVD player to keep kids entertained. Don't forget frequent stops for burning off steam.
- **Keep your eyes open when checking out the sights.** Theme parks and other attractions with long line-ups will often allow kids with disabilities to jump the queue, so be sure to find out about their policies.

Get in Touch

Kéroul
Tourism and culture resources for travelling with a disability, including an accessible Quebec guide.
514-252-3104
www.keroul.qc.ca

Accessible Transportation Directorate
Canadian Transportation Agency
1-888-222-2592
cta.comment@cta-otc.gc.ca
www.cta-otc.gc.ca/access/index_e.html

Access to Travel
Federal government website lists information on travelling with a disability, arranged by province or mode of travel.
www.accesstotravel.gc.ca

Access Guide Canada
An online directory of accessible lodgings, attractions, restaurants, and more across Canada.
www.abilities.ca/agc

General Resources for Getting a Life

Organizations

Mothers Are Women
info@mothersarewomen.com
www.mothersarewomen.com

Web

Womennet.ca: Canadian Women's Virtual Information Centre
www.womennet.ca

Mothers in Motion
Information and support for mothers who want to lead healthy
lifestyles and teach their children to do so as well.
www.caaws.ca/mothersinmotion

Books

*More Than a Mom: Living a Full and Balanced Life When Your
Child Has Special Needs*
By Heather Fawcett and Amy Baskin

Mom Management: Managing Mom Before Everybody Else
By Tracy Lyn Moland
To order, call 403-226-8798
www.tracylynmoland.com

Tax Tips and Financial Savvy 9

Meet Victoria Levack
Berwick, Nova Scotia

Joan Langevin Levack says life was turned on its ear when she met her man and moved in with his two girls nine years ago. Of course, taking on a new husband and two young stepdaughters is a titanic change in itself. But seventeen-year-old Victoria has cerebral palsy, and becoming her primary caregiver has transformed Joan's life in many ways.

For one thing, Joan and Victoria have become extremely close. "Vicky is such a good kid," says Joan. "I like her a lot. She's very funny, like her dad. She's very, very bright."

Their relationship has also opened Joan's eyes when it comes to special needs. "Out of necessity, I've become a real advocate for people with disabilities," says Joan. "We live in rural Nova Scotia, and I spend a lot of time figuring out how to help her."

One thing it didn't take Joan long to learn: Disabilities cost big bucks, and getting Victoria what she needs often means digging down deep into their pockets. "We earn far above the average here," says Joan, "and yet we're always broke." Some examples of expenses: The wheelchair van the family needs to get around in a place with no accessible public transportation, and the medication Vicky takes to ease her hip spasms. Then there's the addition to their home they're financing so that Vicky can finally have the accessible bathroom she's waited years for.

"The other day, my husband figured out that we've spent probably $400 on eating utensils," says Joan. Although their insurance plan sometimes helps out, most of the time at least part of the cost of adaptive devices must come from the Levack family purse. "We had to buy a wheelchair tray that wasn't covered, so that was a couple of hundred bucks," says Joan. "Hell, I've probably spent a couple of hundred bucks just on Velcro!"

Often, the costs of disability are indirect. The Levacks pay to have their long country driveway plowed clear of snow because it's the only way Victoria's school bus can pick her up. Joan shelled out seventy dollars recently for a massage so she wouldn't injure herself lifting Vicky. There's rarely money left over at the end of the month.

Because home care services in their region of Canada are income tested (that is, not offered to households above a certain income threshold), the family isn't eligible for support. "They laughed at me," says Joan. But, unexpectedly, her application for a federal disability benefit went through. Even though the monthly payment they get from the government is modest, "That's made a difference," Joan says.

She's also grateful for the financial help they've received from a local community service group. And when a brand-new, balloon-festooned accessible bicycle was delivered to Victoria courtesy of a non-profit organization that fulfills the dreams of kids with disabilities, it brought tears to Joan's eyes. "Vicky almost died! It was very cool, because that was the kind of thing we just couldn't afford."

Still, the Levacks recognize that they are fortunate compared to many other families who are contending with the costs of special needs. In her job as a disability employment officer, Joan speaks regularly to men and women who are in pretty dire straits. "These are people who can't afford shoes," she says. "People are phoning me and saying, 'They shut my heat off because I needed to buy a brace for my leg.' So it helps to keep it in perspective."

Joan loves her stepdaughters dearly, and like any mom, she's willing to move mountains for them. "The thing is, that's life," she says. "You have kids, you make sacrifices." Judging from the way Joan sprinkles her conversation with references to Victoria's sparkle, wit, and enthusiasm, the sacrifices are worth it. She adores having Vicky in her life, and will cheer for her for the long term. "I want her to keep growing, and have a good life."

No one ever said it was easy, and no one ever said it was cheap. The heavy costs related to raising a child with special needs can sometimes feel like they're breaking the bank. But speaking of breaks, you should know that there are many benefits, tax claims, and discounts that can put a little wherewithal back in your wallet.

The Child Disability Benefit

If you've never heard about the Child Disability Benefit (CDB), now's the time to read all about it. The CDB is a monthly payment you may be eligible to receive from the Government of Canada. While it's no jackpot, it can certainly help offset some of your disability expenses.

There are three questions that will determine whether or not you can get the CDB:

1. **Is your child's disability "severe"?**
    Your child's disability is considered severe if she's "markedly restricted" in her ability to carry out a basic daily activity such as walking, speaking, making appropriate decisions, or going to the bathroom independently.

2. **Is your child's disability "prolonged"?**

   Your child's disability is considered prolonged if it lasts (or will probably last) for more than a year.

3. **What's your household income?**

   The amount you receive per month is calculated using a formula that's based on your household income, as well as the number of children in your family. Unless you're in an extremely high income bracket, you'll receive at least some benefit.

To apply for the CDB, fill out and submit the Disability Tax Credit Certificate (see the info later in this chapter). The Canada Revenue Agency will then decide whether or not you are eligible. If your application is successful, the benefit will be added to your monthly Canada Child Tax Benefit (CCTB) payment.

Do it today! The Canada Revenue Agency accepts CDB forms all through the year, so there's no need to wait until tax time to apply.

Get in Touch

"Child Disability Benefit (CDB)"

Call 1-800-959-8281 for information

Read online at www.cra-arc.gc.ca/benefits/disability-e.html

Provincial Government Benefits

In addition to federal funding, most Canadian provinces offer other benefits to help parents with the costs of raising a child with a disability. These are usually administered through the ministry for community or social services, family and children's services, or the ministry of health. Eligibility criteria and what the programs cover will vary from province to province.

Get in Touch

Disability Support Program
PEI Ministry of Health
902-368-5996
www.gov.pe.ca/hss/peidsp

Family Support Subsidies
Quebec Community Services
Office des personnes handicapées Québec
1-800-567-1465

Assistance for Children with Severe Disabilities
Ontario Ministry of Children and Youth Services
416-325-0500
www.children.gov.on.ca/mcys/english/programs/needs/index.asp
Family Support for Children with Disabilities
Alberta Government Children's Services
780-427-2551
www.child.alberta.ca/home/591.cfm

Services to Children with Disabilities
Yukon Family and Children's Services
867-667-8950
www.hss.gov.yk.ca/programs/family_children

Non-Government Grants and Funds

Big Brother isn't your only source of funding. Many non-government, charitable organizations and foundations in Canada are set up to give financial assistance to families raising kids with special needs. Tracking them down and filling out forms in triplicate, on the other hand, can sometimes be a full-time job in itself! But it's worth the hassle if you can hustle up support. So where to look?

- **Certain charities,** like Jennifer Ashleigh Children's Charity or Variety—The Children's Charity, distribute funds to families who need help covering the costs of specialized equipment or therapies.
- **Disability service organizations,** like Easter Seals and the Spina Bifida and Hydrocephalus Association, will often foot the bill for special services or supplies.
- **Many corporations** operate charitable foundations, like TUPPY'S Children's Foundation (The UPS Store and Mail Boxes Etc.) and President's Choice Children's Charity, that will fund children with special needs.
- **Community service groups** like Kiwanis, Lions, or Rotary Club often donate money or equipment to support families in their neighbourhoods.
- **Your insurance company** may not be so charitable, but you'd be surprised at what it will fund. If you have a medical plan, find out which of your child's disability-related costs are covered.

Get in Touch

Jennifer Ashleigh Children's Charity
905-852-1799
generalmail@jenash.org
www.jenniferashleighfoundation.ca

Variety—The Children's Charity of British Columbia
604-320-0505
info@variety.bc.ca
www.variety.bc.ca

Easter Seals Canada
416-932-8382
info@easterseals.ca
www.easterseals.ca

Family Independence Fund
Vancouver Foundation
604-688-2204
info@vancouverfoundation.bc.ca
www.vancouverfoundation.ca/grants/applyingforpartner.htm

Special Needs Fund
Spina Bifida and Hydrocephalus Association of Nova Scotia
902-679-1124
spina.bifida@ns.sympatico.ca
www.sbhans.ca

TUPPY'S Children's Foundation
The UPS Store and Mail Boxes Etc.
1-800-661-6232, ext. 287
hstafford@theupsstore.ca

President's Choice Charity
1-888-495-5111
www.presidentschoice.ca/ChildrensCharity

Lions Clubs International
Lists Lions Club locations across Canada.
www.lionsclubs.org

House Help

Moving? Renovating? If your child needs accessibility features at home
like a ramp or wheelchair bathroom, here's what you should know:

- **Your moving expenses can be claimed** as a medical expense, if
  you're moving to a house that's more functional for your child.
- **The cost of your renovations can also be claimed,** as long as they
  are being done to accommodate your child's disability. So keep
  those hardware store receipts—and ask contractors to use descrip-
  tive words such as "wheelchair modifications" on their receipts.
- **If your income is modest**, you may be eligible for the Residential
  Rehabilitation Assistance Program for Persons with Disabilities.
  This federal government fund helps low-income homeowners pay
  for adaptations.
- **Your province may also have special funding programs** to help
  with the cost of accessibility modifications. For example, in
  Ontario, the Ontario March of Dimes administers the province's
  Home and Vehicle Modification Program to help homeowners
  below a specified income limit. Check with your province's min-
  istry of health.

Get in Touch

Residential Rehabilitation Assistance Program for Persons with
Disabilities (RRAP-Disabilities)

Canada Mortgage and Housing Corporation (CMHC)

613-748-2000

chic@cmhc-schl.gc.ca

www.cmhc-schl.gc.ca/en/co/prfinas/prfinas_003.cfm

Ontario March of Dimes

1-800-263-3463

www.marchofdimes.ca

Disability Discounts

Just as the costs of your kid's disability can add up, so too can small
windfalls. A savings here or a rebate there can ease some of the
pressure on your purse. When you visit attractions such as muse-
ums or parks, ask about special offers for children with disabilities.
If your kid is applying for college, do your homework—find out if
the school offers bursaries for students who have disabilities. (See
Chapter 10 for more tuition top-ups.) Here are a few leads to get
you started:

- **Canada Study Grant.** Up to $8,000 in federal funds is available
  to post-secondary students with disabilities to cover education
  costs such as computers or notetaking services.
- **Duty-free shopping.** You don't have to pay duty if your order is
  from across the border, provided the item you're purchasing is
  designed for use by someone with a disability.
- **Sales tax rebates.** In many provinces you're exempt from paying
  sales tax on certain disability-related items.
- **Hollywood on the house.** The free Access 2 Entertainment

Card, accepted by major theatre chains, gets your child into the movies either free or at a discount.

- **Free parking.** Many municipalities across Canada, although not all, allow free parking at meters if you have a disability permit. If you're not sure about your community's bylaws, check with your local traffic division.

Get in Touch

National Student Loan Service Centre, Public Institution Division
1-888-815-4514

Customs Information
Canada Border Services Agency
1-800-461-9999

Access 2 Entertainment
416-932-8382, ext. 227
info@access2.ca
www.access2.ca

Save the Secondhand Way

Often, equipment and supplies carry a hefty price tag. And kids outgrow some items faster than you can say, "Does that come with adjustable footrests?" One way to save is to go secondhand. Used and reconditioned wheelchairs and other aids are rented or sold at a low cost by some service organizations. Even your local equipment dealer may sell secondhand devices. You can also check out disability classifieds online.

Get in Touch

Children's Wheelchair Recycling Program
Abilities Foundation of Nova Scotia
902-453-6000
www.abilitiesfoundation.ns.ca

Special Needs Equipment Exchange Service
Disabled Persons Community Resources
613-724-5886
www.dpcr.ca

Canadian Paraplegic Association Swap and Shop Classified Ads
www.canparaplegic.org/en/204

Tax Time

This may be a painful and even depressing time of year, but income tax is a necessary evil. Turn it to your advantage: By learning all you can about tax credits and claimable expenses, you'll put more pesos back into your own pocket.

The Disability Tax Credit

If your child has a "severe and prolonged" disability according to the definitions on page 163, be sure to fill out and submit the Disability Tax Credit Certificate, Form T2201. Not only will a successful application mean getting a monthly Child Disability Benefit, but you'll also get a Disability Tax Credit when you're completing your income tax. The exact amount of the credit changes every year (check the General Income Tax Guide for the year to find out the amount). As long as your child has no income of his own, the credit can be transferred to you as a supporting parent.

The Disability Tax Credit Certificate must be signed by a qualified professional, such as your child's doctor. Certain other professionals like audiologists can also sign the form, as long as their area of expertise relates to your child's disability.

Medical Expense Tax Credit

Have you been doling out dough for drugs, devices, and doctors? A portion of some of your child's disability-related expenses can be claimed as medical expenses. There's a formula that determines what portion you can claim. Multiply this portion by the tax rate percentage specified for the year, and you have calculated your medical expense tax credit.

Don't think your kid's costs will qualify? Think again! Although some eligible expenses are no-brainers—like wheelchairs, hearing aids, and orthopedic shoes—others are less obvious. Here are just a few examples of unexpected medical expenses you may be able to claim. (Note: For some of them, a doctor's prescription is required.) So be sure to save those receipts!

- special diapers
- communication boards
- air conditioners
- computer software
- tutoring of a child with learning disabilities
- the extra costs of gluten-free foods
- expenses for special skills dogs
- cost of specialized training so you (or a relative) can care for your kid

Gold Star Idea

If you are casting about for a new financial expert to help with your income tax return, make sure she has some knowledge of disability issues. Ask her if she has many clients with disabilities, or get referrals from other parents with families like yours. A professional who specializes in special needs will have the expertise to find you write-offs and refunds that another tax preparer could easily overlook. Every copper counts!

Get in Touch
Canada Revenue Agency
1-800-959-8281
www.cra-arc.gc.ca

"What Can People with Disabilities Claim as a Deduction or Credit?"
Canada Revenue Agency
Read online at www.cra-arc.gc.ca/tax/individuals/segments/ disabilities/deductions

"Income Tax Preparation Regarding Learning Disabilities"
Learning Disabilities Association of B.C., Vancouver Chapter
Read online at www.ldav.ca/adv_tax.html

Fighting for Fairness
A website maintained by an advocate for fairness in the tax system for Canadians with disabilities.
www.disabilitytaxcredit.com

Tax Tips and Financial Savvy

In a Tizzy? Quick Tax Tips

If you're like most parents of kids with special needs, you probably have enough paper on file to redecorate the walls of your living room. Here are a few strategies for making sure you've got the documents you need. (Admittedly, these ideas won't reduce your paper load—but it may help you organize it.)

- **Keep everything together.** It may sound simple, but have you ever turned your den upside down trying to turn up one particular invoice or statement? Dedicate part of a filing drawer or cabinet to keeping your papers in one place.
- **Get a system.** Different methods will work for different people. Find one you can dance to. Here's one suggestion: Use four or five clearly labelled folders for the current year so you can file documents immediately as you collect them. Categories might include medical expenses, household expenses, financial statements, and application forms.
- **When in doubt, don't throw it out.** If you're not sure whether or not you'll be able to claim an expense, keep that receipt on file and consult with your accountant at tax time.
- **Ask your babysitter for receipts.** If you pay for someone to watch your child while you work or go to school—even if it's your next-door neighbour—get a receipt and claim the expense on your tax return. Day camp counts, too, if you use it for day care.
- **Get in line for the new Children's Fitness Tax Credit.** You can now claim the fees you pay when you sign your sprout up for physical activities like gymnastics, swimming, or soccer. Kids with disabilities, in particular, are eligible for this tax credit for an extra two years (up to age 18).
- **Keep your ear to the ground.** The Canada Revenue Agency frequently announces other new credits. Listen to the news, visit the CRA website, or check in with your accountant to learn about changes that can, well, save you change. An example is the

new Tax Credit for Public Transit Passes, which lets you claim the cost of your kid's bus pass.

- **Backclaim expenses from the previous year.** Did you discover an old drugstore receipt you forgot to claim last year? Save it for your tax preparer this year.
- **Don't count on computer records.** These days it's not uncommon for companies to send receipts by email—after all, it saves them a stamp. But be sure to make your own printout for your files in case your computer suddenly goes to hardware heaven.
- **Be a packrat...for at least six years.** Canada Revenue Agency requires you to hold on to your tax records for at least six years. (Fun fact: You actually need *written permission* from your regional tax office if you want to destroy your records before this time limit.)

Financial Planning for the Future

Ever think about your child's income down the road? Put your trust in a trust! If your kid continues to receive government benefits as an adult, he may have a limit on the assets he's allowed to keep. This can pose a problem. For instance, what if he wants to save up for a splurge, like a big-screen TV or a furniture set? And how do you leave him a lump sum in your will? A fat bank account can jeopardize his monthly income.

But a trust is different. Money that's set up in a trust and disbursed to your child for specific purposes may not necessarily be deducted from his provincial government benefits. A lawyer with expertise in trusts and disabilities can help you set up a trust with your child as the beneficiary. This way, you can steer clear of the cash clawback.

If you don't yet have a will, what are you waiting for? No one thinks of estate planning as big fun. But if you die without a will, your estate will be distributed as the government sees fit—and not necessarily according to your wishes. When you have a kid with a disability, it's critical that you have a say in important issues like guardianship and bequests.

For more on your child's future, see Chapter 10.

Get in Touch
"Succession Planning for Families with Disabled Dependants"
The Knowledge Bureau
Read online at
www.knowledgebureau.com/enNewsBureauArticle.asp?id=530

Kenneth C. Pope, LL.B, TEP
Practises in Ontario and interprovincially in disability-related
estate planning and tax matters. Resource materials and initial
consults are free upon request.
1-866-536-7673
kpope@kpopelaw.ca
www.kpopelaw.ca

*Removing the Mystery: An Estate Planning Guide for Families
of People with Disabilities*
By Graeme Treeby
In CD-ROM format or paper copy.
Available from the Ontario Federation for Cerebral Palsy
416-244-9686
www.ofcp.on.ca/ltp_resources.html

"Tips on Estate Planning for Special Needs Families"
By Brett Langill
Read online at www.bloorview.ca/resourcecentre/
familyresources/estateplanning.php

The Wills Book
Information on benefits, wills, and trusts for people with dis-
abilities.
By Mary Louise Dickson and Rod Walsh

Available from Community Living Ontario

416-447-4348

www.communitylivingontario.ca/forsale.html

.

"How to Prepare Your Will"

By Mary L. MacGregor

Read online at www.bloorview.ca/resourcecentre/

familyresources/preparingyourwill.php

General Resources for Money Matters

Web

Canada Benefits

Links Canadians to government benefits for which they might be eligible. Site includes an interactive "Benefits Finder" that assesses your eligibility.

www.canadabenefits.gc.ca

"If a Piggy Bank Could Talk... A Financial Guide for Canadian Families"

MasterCard Canada and the Credit Counselling Service of Canada

Read online at www.mastercard.com/ca/wce/PDF/

10754_MC-Financial-Guide.pdf

Books

Cheap Talk with the Frugal Friends: Over 600 Tips, Tricks, and Creative Ideas for Saving Money

By Angie Zalewski and Deana Ricks

Preparing for the Future 10

Meet Brent Wilson
Coquitlam, British Columbia

Brent is thirty years old. He loves to ski in winter, and has recently taken up sailing in summer. He works at a video store and a pub. He's been known to jet to Mexico for his holidays. He enjoys music and parties, and is always happy to raise a pint with his buddies.

Brent moved away from home a year and a half ago. He relishes his independence, although Mom and Dad dearly miss having him at home. No matter. They know their son is happy. And that's what counts.

"We just want Brent to have a full life," says his mom. Brent grew up with a developmental disability and has also dealt with chronic illness for many years. He's non-verbal so, to communicate, he uses sign language and a personalized communication book. Brent has some difficulty using his hands and relies on support staff to help with fiddly tasks like buttons and shaving.

Brent's parents, Debbie and Randy, have always been there to see him through the highs and the lows. The lows have meant years of hospitalizations and treatments that almost knocked the stuffing out of him. But the highs have included going on a three-day camping trip with his classmates, and celebrating high school graduation with his friends, complete with fancy tux and limousine service.

Debbie and Randy have always worked hard to make sure that Brent was included at school and in the community. The job didn't stop when Brent finished high school.

When Brent's parents looked at the opportunities for a young adult with disabilities in their community, they realized it was up to them to come up with some new ones. Otherwise, their son might have nothing to look forward to but supervised day programs, where he'd be segregated along with other adults with disabilities.

For Debbie and Randy, this wasn't an option. "That's not what we wanted for Brent," says Debbie. "We had fought so hard for inclusion, it would be a step backwards."

Instead they set up what's known as a Vela microboard for Brent. A microboard is a bona fide but small-scale non-profit organization that is eligible for funding, and supports someone with a disability to realize his life goals and dreams. (Find out more at www.microboard.org.) Brent's parents stocked the board of directors with family and friends who know him personally and care about his future.

Then they contemplated what to name it. Randy suggested the Don't-Leave-Me-in-Front-of-the-TV Society. They settled on the Brent Wilson Choices and Opportunities Society. For eleven years and counting, the microboard has helped Brent identify his interests and shape his life direction.

Debbie and Randy couldn't be happier with Brent's new living arrangements. Surely it was serendipity: Brent's close friend and former support worker bought a house nearby, built a suite for Brent, and invited him to live with his family, which includes two small girls. "At first I was hesitant. Brent is really nervous around little children because they're unpredictable. I didn't know how it was going to go," says Debbie. "But he has such a special relationship with the older daughter, who's four. She's learned some sign language." Brent takes his meals with the family—not a bad deal when you consider that his friend is now a trained chef. And through his microboard, he continues to hire staff to support him with personal tasks, his job, and volunteer work.

What does Debbie see down the road? She is counting on the fact that the Brent Wilson Choices and Opportunities Society will be there for him long after she and Randy are gone. Not long ago, Brent's younger brother Todd asked to join the board. This close circle of supporters has made such a difference that Randy and Debbie have already established a microboard for their daughter Roxanne, who has Down syndrome.

In the meantime, Debbie is thrilled with the path her oldest child is taking. "It's my fairy-tale ending, to have him living with people he knows and love him," she says.

"He is just so happy."

It seems like only yesterday that you were the hand that rocks the cradle. But if you're reading this chapter, it's because your cherub is growing fast. It's time to look ahead. After all, many of the supports and services your sweetie has been relying on for years may very well fall away when she hits the magic ages of 18 or 21.

Life is going to change, and you want it to be the best it can be for your kid. From puberty to post-secondary school, from employment to estate planning, this chapter will help you set your sights on the years ahead.

The Planet of Puberty

Help! That sweet-smelling baby with the silky skin you used to gobble like candy has been replaced by something hairy and stinking like a goat! Whether or not your kid has special needs, the onset of puberty can sometimes make him seem like he's from another galaxy. His body changes, his social circle shifts, and his moods swings are wilder than a monkey in a banana tree. For a variety of reasons, a disability often complicates the situation.

What changes can you expect at adolescence?

- **Body changes**. Surely you remember the growing, the deepening, the swelling, and the thickening.
- **Social changes**. Some adolescents with special needs start spending more time alone. Be on the lookout for social isolation.
- **Mood changes.** Shifts in hormone levels can cause your upbeat little buddy to crash down or lash out. But don't confuse normal mood swings with depression, which may need to be treated. Watch for low self-esteem, insomnia, and withdrawal from hobbies or family.

All of these changes require some explaining. That's where you come in. Here are some strategies for tackling adolescent topics:

- **Don't delay.** Don't wait too long to talk about bodily changes and menstruation. Some kids develop early—girls can have their first period as early as nine or ten. Children with spina bifida and hydrocephalus are more likely to start puberty early.
- **Discuss puberty in private.** This helps to teach your child that many of these issues—like breast development, pubic hair, and periods—are also private.
- **Be calm, positive, and open.** Make your child understand that growing up is normal and wonderful (even if, privately, you're not ready for it to happen!).
- **Use proper language.** Don't refer to your daughter's "yoo-hoo" or your son's "wing-wang." At best, it's confusing. At worst, it implies that these body parts are shameful and shouldn't be called by their correct names.

- **Use props.** Puppets or dolls can be helpful when explaining body changes or functions.
- **Break it down.** If your child is having trouble understanding something, explain the basics in bite-sized pieces.
- **Let him ask questions.** Use a book or pictures if you're uncomfortable coming up with answers on your own.
- **Be prepared to review.** Don't think of the big talk as a one-time event. Your child will likely need ongoing guidance as new issues crop up, or reminders may be in order.

Help with Hygiene

Keeping your child's body clean becomes even more important at adolescence, so help her learn a daily routine. Keep pictures in the bathroom to remind her of the steps. Make sure she's using deodorant, washing her hair frequently enough, washing her face, and wearing clean clothes.

Speaking of Sex

It may not be easy to think of your child as a sexual being. But sexuality is a fundamental part of every one of us. Of course, society has long subscribed to the myth that people with disabilities aren't interested in sex—but any horny teenager will tell you that's simply not true!

As your child comes of age, you may be tempted to avoid talking about sex in order to protect her. The truth is, it works the other way around: Teaching her about sex, appropriate behaviour, and her rights will actually go a long way towards keeping her safe.

As you review the facts of life with your child, here are five facts to keep straight for yourself:

1. **If your child is asking, she's ready for answers.** Don't avoid the topic or say, "I'll tell you when you're older." Of course, she may not need all the gory details at an early stage. Keep your answers age-appropriate but honest.

2. **If your child *isn't* asking, that doesn't mean he's *not* ready for answers.** Your child might be embarrassed to cover the topic with you. Or he might think he knows it all. That doesn't mean you shouldn't go there.

3. **There's no such thing as a sexuality disability.** Whether your child has autism, epilepsy, learning disabilities, or heart disease, that won't stop her from having sexual thoughts and feelings.

4. **Teens with special needs aren't sterile.** Bear in mind that most disabilities do not affect a person's ability to make babies. And they definitely don't give immunity to STDs.

5. **Guess what? Not all people with disabilities are straight.** If your child is gay, she faces the challenge of belonging to two minority groups—and will sometimes feel like she's not fully included in either. Fortunately, there's a growing number of resources for gay people with disabilities.

Get in Touch

"Disability and Sexuality: Getting Ready to Talk About It"
Bloorview Kids Rehab
Read online at www.bloorview.ca/resourcecentre/
familyresources/sexuality.php

"Disability and Sexuality"
Spiderbytes.ca
www.spiderbytes.ca/Sexuality/Sexuality_Disability.shtml

Sexuality: Your Sons and Daughters with Intellectual Disabilities
By Karin Melberg Schwier and David Hingsburger

Caution: Do Not Open Until Puberty! An Introduction to Sexuality for Young Adults with Disabilities
By Rick Enright
Available from the Thames Valley Children's Centre
519-685-8680
www.tvcc.on.ca/caution-do-not-open-until-puberty.htm

Autism-Asperger's & Sexuality: Puberty and Beyond
By Jerry and Mary Newport

SHADE Consulting Ltd.
Vancouver, B.C.
Offers workshops for parents of children with disabilities on sex ed–themed topics, such as, "Help! We've Hit Puberty!"
604-434-9579
info@shadeconsulting.ca
www.shadeconsulting.ca

Queers On Wheels
A U.S. organization serving people with disabilities in the GLBTQ (gay, lesbian, bisexual, transgender, or queer) community.
info@queesonwheels.com
www.queersonwheels.com

Ontario Rainbow Alliance of the Deaf
info@orad.ca
www.orad.ca

Reducing the Risks

Sadly, children with special needs face a higher risk of abuse than other kids. One alarming B.C. study showed that high school students with chronic conditions were twice as likely to have been sexually assaulted as their able-bodied peers. But you can take steps to protect your child. Here are six critical lessons to teach your kid:

1. **Teach boundaries.** When it comes to her body, she rules. Any part of her body that's normally covered by a bathing suit is private. But even if she doesn't want so much as a shoulder pat, she's the boss.
2. **Teach "no."** Children with disabilities often learn to be compliant as they are poked and prodded by health professionals or told what to do by teachers. Do some role playing: Have your child practise saying "no" in a forceful voice.
3. **Teach privacy for playtime.** It's natural for your not-so-little one to seek a little personal pleasure. The rule is simple: Masturbation is normal and healthy, but it belongs in the bedroom.
4. **Teach appropriate behaviour.** You used to think it was cute when your six-year-old ran up to complete strangers and hugged them. But now that she's a developing twelve-year-old, it may be time to rein in those displays of affection.
5. **Teach dating safety.** If your teen is ready for dating, teach her basic safety tips such as dating in groups, meeting in public places, introducing her date to you, and carrying a cellphone.
6. **Teach cyber security.** Tell your teen never to give out personal details when he's online, such as where he lives or goes to school.

Get in Touch
Just Say Know! Understanding and Reducing the Risk of Sexual Victimization of People with Developmental Disabilities
By Dave Hingsburger
Available from Diverse City Press
latourdcp@hotmail.com
www.diverse-city.com

Sexuality—Preparing Your Child with Special Needs: How to Develop a Plan for Sex Education and Sexual Abuse Protection
Developmental Disabilities Resource Center on Sexuality (U.S.)
Read online at www.moddrc.com/

Time for Transitions!

Puberty isn't the only time of change for your child. Coming of age also means leaving behind longtime supports like public school, therapy, programming—and, yes, even devoted moms and dads. Depending on your child's abilities and inclinations, he may be headed for college, a job, a place of his own. Even if he does none of those things, like all young adults he'll likely want to live as independently as he can. Don't wait until he's seventeen and a half to start preparing him for age eighteen.

Many rehabilitation facilities and children's treatment centres offer teen independence programs—specialty camps or programs that can provide concrete training to kids with disabilities who are coming of age. Typically, they take place with peers, and they're barrels of fun.

Get in Touch

Teen Independence Camp
Adolescent & Young Adult Program
G.F. Strong Rehab Centre
Vancouver, B.C.
604-734-1313, ext. 6225

Teen Independence Week
Child Health Program
Janeway Child Health Centre

St. John's, Newfoundland
709-777-4418

 ## Gold Star Idea

Want your child to gain independence as she grows up? Think ahead! Starting early, give your child household chores. Teach her to make restaurant reservations or book her own haircuts. Encourage her to make her own decisions and develop her own interests. This approach will better equip her as she becomes an adult.

Post-Secondary School

If your child is hankering for a higher education, be heartened: Universities and colleges offer a good array of services to students with disabilities. Not only are school campuses more wheelchair accessible than they've ever been, but they're well endowed with support services as well. Does your daughter have a learning disability? She can receive extra supervised time to complete exams. Does she require assistive devices? These can be provided. Is she unable to take notes? Notetaking services are available. Once your child contacts the school's department for disability services, they'll work with her to determine appropriate academic accommodations.

And there's no need to stop there when it comes to networking. A great way for your child to make the grade is by joining the club! Unions of students with disabilities can be a valuable source of peer support for fretful freshmen. They can also influence on-campus improvements, provide information and resources, and create social opportunities.

Get in Touch

A Family Affair: Preparing Parents and Students with Learning Disabilities for Postsecondary Education; and
Together for Success: A Road Map for Postsecondary Students with Learning Disabilities
Titles available from the Learning Disabilities Association of Canada
613-238-5721
www.ldac-taac.ca

"Navigating Law School and Beyond: A Practical Guide for Students Who Have Disabilities"
Reach Canada
Read online at
www.reach.ca/images/Navigating_Law_School.pdf

Your Education—Your Future
An online guide to college and university for students with psychiatric disabilities.
www.cmha.ca/youreducation

National Educational Association for Disabled Students (NEADS)
613-526-8008
info@neads.ca
www.neads.ca

l'Association québécoise inter-universitaire des conseillers pour les étudiants ayant des besoins spéciaux (AQICEBS)
aqicebs@aqicebs.qc.ca
www.aqicebs.qc.ca

Disability Resource Network of BC
Advocates for people with disabilities in post-secondary education.

604-443-8438
wmcniven@vcc.ca
www.drnbc.org

Adaptech
Research findings, inexpensive downloads, and resources for students with disabilities.
www.adaptech.org

Directory of Campus Groups/Committees of Students with Disabilities
National Educational Association for Disabled Students
www.neads.ca/en/norc/campusnet/groups.php

Show Me the Money

Hitting the books can take big bucks, and post-secondary education is more costly than ever in Canada. For families of students with disabilities, who already contend with extra expenses, coming up with tuition fees can be a trial. Fortunately, many bursaries and grants are aimed at students with special needs. And the best part? No payback. Since the application process is often through the province's student loans program, that's the best place to start—as well as your child's school's financial aid office.

Get in Touch
Canada Access Grant for Students with Permanent Disabilities
Human Resources and Skills Development Canada
For more info, call National Student Loan Service Centre, Public Institution Division
1-888-815-4514
www.hrsdc.gc.ca/en/learning/canada_student_loan/grant2.shtml

Financial Aid Directory
National Educational Association for Disabled Students
www.neads.ca/en/norc/funding

National Bursary Program
Spina Bifida and Hydrocephalus Association of Canada
1-800-565-9488
www.sbhac.ca

Tanabe Bursary
Cerebral Palsy Association of British Columbia
604-515-9455
info@bccerebralpalsy.com
www.bccerebralpalsy.com/pdfs/cpabc_bursary.pdf

MuchMoreMusic AccessAbility Scholarship
A $5,000 scholarship for students with disabilities to support
tuition toward a career in broadcasting.
www.muchmoremusic.com/scholarship

Canada Millennium Scholarship Foundation
Awards bursaries to students in financial need.
www.millenniumscholarships.ca

Scholarships Canada.com
An online database of scholarships and student bursaries.
www.scholarshipscanada.com

The Working Life

Some youths with disabilities opt for employment when they leave
high school or college. In many ways, they're just like other young job
seekers: They lack a lot of experience or specialized skills. But for kids

with special needs, whose free time as teenagers may have been consumed by therapy, tutoring, or daily care, their résumés are even more meager. So how do you give your young worker wannabe an edge?

- **Starting in high school,** help your child hook into volunteer opportunities. These jobs are easier to land than paid positions, look good on a résumé, and provide a chance to network and gain references. They also give your child a chance to explore his likes and dislikes in a job.
- **Sign your child up** with disability organizations that offer transition-to-work programs. Not only will they help your child develop employment skills and gain job experience, they may even help her find a permanent position.
- **Tap into your own network.** The vast majority of job openings are never advertised. Pass the word among your friends, colleagues, and relatives that your child is looking for work.
- **Seek out summer student grants.** Some provincial and federal government programs will partially or fully fund the wages of a student with a disability working in a summer job. Naturally, this gives an employer more incentive to hire your kid.
- **Get a job coach.** Sometimes the same service agencies that helped you pay for a caregiver when your kid was small will also supply support staff to accompany your young adult on the job.

Get in Touch
Transition from School to Work: Career Choices for Youth with Disabilities
Available from the National Educational Association for Disabled Students
613-526-8008
www.neads.ca

Employment Connections: A Transition Tool Kit for Youth with Disabilities
Read online at www.neads.ca/en/about/projects/
student_leadership/employment_connections

NEADS Online Work System
An online job registry for post-secondary students and graduates with disabilities.
www.nows.ca

WORKink
Online employment resource centre for job seekers with disabilities.
www.workink.com

Ability Online Job Readiness Program
Free online program for young adults with disabilities who are planning careers or preparing for job interviews.
1-866-650-6207
www.abilityonline.org

Ability Edge
Offers an internship program across Canada for graduates with disabilities who want to work.
1-888-507-3343
info@abilityedge.ca
www.abilityedge.ca

Canada Summer Jobs
Provides wage subsidies for students facing barriers (like disabilities) to getting summer jobs.
Call 1-800-935-5555 for more information
www1.servicecanada.gc.ca/en/epb/yi/yep/programs/scpp.shtml

Mo' Money

Don't forget to count your kid at tax time. Although you can no longer receive the Child Disability Benefit once he turns eighteen, you may now be able to claim other amounts, such as the Caregiver Amount, or the Amount for Infirm Dependants Age 18 or Older.

Once your child becomes an adult, there are deductions that he can claim as well. For instance, your child can claim a Disability Supports Deduction if he paid for services or devices that he needed in order to work or attend school. Eligible expenses include attendant care, job coaching services, computer software, and sign language interpretation.

Get in Touch
Canada Revenue Agency
"Medical and Disability-Related Information"
1-800-959-8281
www.cra-arc.gc.ca/E/pub/tg/rc4064/README.html

The Future Is Now... Or Anyway, It's Coming

Whether or not our kids have disabilities, we all want the same things for their future: happiness and health, safety and security. Chapter 9 touches on financial considerations for your kid's future. But what about those less tangible targets, like personal fulfillment and caring friendships, winter vacations and a warm hearth at home? How do you ensure your child will live a good life? Hopefully you've already started developing your dreams for him. Perhaps he's shared his with you. As your child grows up, it's time to put plans into action.

It's a fact that you won't be here forever. In decades past, kids with special needs seldom outlived their parents. Not so today. Depending on your child's disability, he may always need some level of support to live a full life. While some adults with disabilities do move to group home settings or chronic care hospitals, many families prefer their grown children to stay in the community, connected to their neighbours and friends.

The idea may seem overwhelming. Fortunately, there are supportive movements and organizations that can help you take charge and lay plans. These resources can assist with important issues like where your child might live, who might care for him, and how he might take part in his community. Often this involves establishing a personal network or circle of friends, relatives, and community members who can commit to a long-term relationship with your kid. Many aging parents have found comfort and joy in these personal networks, knowing their adult children will always have loving supporters in their lives.

Pearl from a Parent

"We're looking to other like-minded families for good ideas about creating an interesting, happy, and challenging life for our son. He is thirty-three; he needs a lot of support, but we have to always be mindful and remind ourselves that he is a grown man. We have written a trust that has some specific instructions about how we would like to think his life will carry on without us."

Get in Touch

PLAN (Planned Lifetime Advocacy Network)
Helps families committed to planning a good life for their loved one with a disability.
604-439-9566
inquiries@plan.ca
www.plan.ca

The Ties that Bind
Website displays Canadian resources and news related to planning a meaningful future for a relative with a disability. DVD
film is also available.
www.tiesthatbind.ca

Families for a Secure Future
905-770-2819
www.familiesforasecurefuture.com

The Road Ahead Society of Calgary
403-263-8226
families@theroadahead.ca
www.theroadahead.ca

Vela Microboard Association
Surrey, B.C.
604-575-2588
info@microboard.org
www.microboard.org

A Good Life: For You and Your Relative with a Disability
By Al Etmanski
Available from PLAN (contact info on page 195)

Peace of Mind
An interactive CD-ROM to help Canadians plan for the future of
their loved one.
Available from PLAN (contact info on page 195)

The Company of Others: Stories of Belonging
By Sandra Shields and David Campion
Available from PLAN (contact info on page 195)

Laying Community Foundations for Your Child with a Disability: How to Establish Relationships that Will Support Your Child after You're Gone
By Linda J. Stengle

What about Brothers and Sisters?

Does your child's future include her siblings? If so, how involved will they be? Will they check in on her a couple times a year, or will they invite her to dinner every day? It's impossible to predict the degree to which her brothers and sisters will look out for her after you're gone. But here are a few strategies for cementing their bond.

- **Start early.** While they're still young, demonstrate your expectation that all your kids are responsible for each other. Have them help each other with household chores or homework.
- **Talk to them as teens**. As your other children get older, speak to them about the future of their sibling with special needs. Share your dreams for him. As they grow into young adults, ask them what they want for their brother or sister.
- **Relegate the right roles.** Don't expect your kids to be full-time caregivers when you're gone. That may not be what's best for anyone. But do consider having them play a key role, like power of attorney, in their sibling's future.

Pearl from a Parent

"As our son's siblings have grown up, we have been very careful to keep them up to date on their brother's life. As they have gotten older we've asked them for more input involving larger issues. In the back of our mind lurks the question: What will happen to our son if something happens to us? How will they step up and be more supportive and involved? Both of them are living far from us, but about three times a year, we have a little state-of-the-union talk to make sure they are up on our dreams for our son, and we get their input about ideas. In the meantime, we do lots of email stories and photos. Also, we get them on iChat so they can see each other on a regular basis, too—even if it's just to call each other butthead!"

General Resources for Coming of Age

Organizations

Family Support Institute
Vancouver, B.C.
Offers workshops to families of people with disabilities, including those addressing the transition to adulthood.
1-800-441-5403
fsi@bcacl.org
www.familysupportbc.com

Best Buddies Canada
Brings together high school students with and without intellectual disabilities to form supportive friendships.
1-888-779-0061
info@bestbuddies.ca
www.bestbuddies.ca

Web

D.O.O.R. 2 Adulthood:
Disability Ontario Online Resource for Transition to Adulthood
www.ablelink.org/public/transition/default.htm

"Tipsheet on Preparing for Transition"
Bloorview Kids Rehab
Read online at www.bloorview.ca/resourcecentre/
familyresources/transitionadulthood.php

"School to Life Transition Handbook"
By Rita McLeod
Saskatchewan Association for Community Living
Read online at www.sasked.gov.sk.ca

Diverse City Press
www.diverse-city.com

Books

Easy for You to Say: Q & As for Teens Living with Chronic Illness or Disability
By Miriam Kaufman

On My Own: A Resource Guide for Living Independently
Guides young people with disabilities in the transition to independence.
Available from the Canadian Abilities Foundation
416-923-1885
www.abilities.ca

Life Skills Activities for Secondary Students with Special Needs
By Darlene Mannix

Freaks, Geeks and Asperger Syndrome: A User Guide to Adolescence
By Luke Jackson

Talking Teenagers: Information and Inspiration for Parents of Teenagers with Autism or Asperger's Syndrome
By Ann Boushey

Life Beyond the Classroom: Transition Strategies for Young People with Disabilities
By Paul Wehman
Available from Brookes Publishing
410-337-9580
www.brookespublishing.com

After Disability: A Guide to Getting on with Life
By Lisa Bendall
(This author's name may sound familiar!) *After Disability* was written to guide adults with disabilities with tips and resources as they source out a place to live, find a job, do their taxes, travel, and pursue recreational activities.

Index

Index